The 10 Cardinal Sins of Leadership

The 10 Cardinal Sins of Leadership

What Thought Leaders Must Never Do to Succeed in High-Risk Environments

Casey J. Bedgood

CRC Press
Taylor & Francis Group
Boca Raton London New York

CRC Press is an imprint of the
Taylor & Francis Group, an **informa** business

A PRODUCTIVITY PRESS BOOK

First published 2022
by Routledge
605 Third Avenue, New York, NY 10158

and by Routledge
4 Park Square, Milton Park, Abingdon, Oxon, OX14 4RN

Routledge is an imprint of the Taylor & Francis Group, an informal business

© 2022 Casey J. Bedgood

Library of Congress Cataloguing-in-Publication Data
A catalog record for this title has been requested

ISBN: 978-1-032-21349-1 (hbk)
ISBN: 978-1-032-21346-0 (pbk)
ISBN: 978-1-003-26796-6 (ebk)

DOI: 10.4324/9781003267966

Typeset in Garamond
by MPS Limited, Dehradun

Contents

Preface

Is risk a reality or just a mirage? Is risk applicable to all industries and businesses? Is everything high-risk, or are some organizational attributes lower-risk? Is it possible to predict the future using current risk environments? Is past risk a good predictor of future risk? Will risk affect the organization and its customers, or just leaders? Are leaders all-knowing? Is ignorance bliss? Is leadership perception always reality? Will leadership ignorance eventually cause organizational failure? Is risk applicable to planning, time, value, knowledge, vision, conflict, perspective, and inclusion efforts? Are there cardinal sins that leaders should avoid, risk-assess, or mitigate if no other options are available? Will leaders truly be knowledgeable of the current state and potential pitfalls if they don't measure risk? We will answer these considerations and others in the following chapters.

The purpose of this book is to provide a custom road map for leaders, aspiring leaders, students, and anyone interested in the art of leadership to succeed in high-risk environments. Often, leaders don't know what they don't know. One main culprit is the lack of assessing, measuring, analyzing, and addressing risk. Simply put, we don't know what we don't measure.

In today's world, change is the only constant. As change grows and evolves, so does risk. If leaders don't understand risk, they and their organizations will surely be disrupted. As Hosea (4:6) wrote, 'My people are destroyed for a lack of knowledge.'

The key to addressing risk is knowledge. As we will learn in the following chapters, perception is not always reality. What leaders think they know, often turns out to be a mirage instead of reality. Also, ignorance is never bliss. What leaders don't know can and will eventually hurt them. This knowledge deficit will also impact organizations and ultimately, their customers.

The key is to address the elephant in the room. But how will leaders address risk if they don't understand its prevalence, scope, impact, and footprint? In short, they won't.

The genesis of this book is over two decades of thought leadership experience. During this time, I have witnessed many leaders at every level struggle to identify, analyze, and address problems. Often, leaders see a problem and go after it. Unfortunately, they play the endless game of 'whack a mole' until they or their organization is disrupted. As a result, the leaders struggle to succeed, are constantly challenged for results, quality of life on the job and off is less-than-desirable, and what could be a great ride often turns into a nightmare.

At the core of it all is risk. Risk is far-reaching. It can be very dangerous and must be mitigated or prevented at every turn. If leaders partake in any of the 10 cardinal sins of thought leadership outlined here, they will realize quickly that their careers will be a series of never-ending potholes instead of a bliss-filled joyride.

About the Author

Casey J. Bedgood is the author of ***The Ideal Performance Improvement Eco System: Quick Guide to Improvement Made Easy*** and ***The Ride of a Lifetime: Seeing The Impossible Become Reality***. He is a healthcare leader with over 20 years of experience. Casey is a Six Sigma Black Belt and accomplished author. Over the years, Casey's work has been recognized, sourced, and modeled by National and Global best practice organizations in the healthcare industry and beyond. He has amassed a portfolio of dozens of publications on topics such as thought leadership, knowledge transfer, performance improvement, strategic design, innovative thinking, transformation, Quality Management System (QMS), and many others. Subsequently, many large complex healthcare enterprises across the US, Canada, and Singapore have sourced and sought after Casey's thought leadership expertise.

Casey earned a BBA Magna Cum Laude from Mercer University and a Master of Public Administration degree from Georgia College & State University (GCSU). He is an IISE Lean Green Belt, Six Sigma Green Belt and Six Sigma Black Belt. Also, Casey has been Change Acceleration Process (CAP) trained via GE, and he is a member of the American College of Healthcare Executives (ACHE).

About the Author

Chapter 1

Planning: The Cardinal Sin of Not Having a Plan

Three Arrows Thought Leaders Must Have in Their Quiver to Succeed

Leadership & Its Challenges

Leadership, formally defined, is the 'capacity to lead.'[1] In layman's terms, leadership is getting others to do what you desire without force. Are all leaders truly leaders? The short answer is not necessarily. Leadership credibility is not and should not be measured based on a person's title, salary, number of direct reports or years in a certain position. Peter Drucker may have defined leadership best by saying, 'Leaders are those that have followers.' Without followers, leaders are irrelevant and lead with title only, which is never a winning strategy.

So why is leadership so important? In recent years, change has become the new norm; the only constant seems to be increasing pace and impact. In healthcare, for example, the last few years have been riddled with historical changes that have altered the industry's trajectory forever. Pre-COVID-19, the industry experienced record number of financial challenges, evidenced by progressively declining revenues and rising costs.

Moreover, the healthcare industry has been and continues to be mired with record consolidation.[2] Across the US, hospitals and health systems have combined at record pace via mergers, acquisitions, and other strategic

DOI: 10.4324/9781003267966-1

combinations. The million-dollar question is why? In short, financial, market, and other regulatory pressures have forced healthcare leaders to find innovative channels or economies of scale to buffer the pressures previously mentioned.

Another and equally important change has been record-level top leadership disruption in healthcare. For nearly the last decade, hospital CEO circles have experienced the highest levels of consistent turnover in decades.[3] This trend has not shown any sign of slowing down in the near future. You may be wondering, what drivers have and continue to contribute to this disruption? The simple answer is there are several drivers, such as natural attrition due to retirements, and market forces such as financial downturns, that have forced underperforming leaders out of their roles and organizational combinations, just to name a few.

So why does this matter in today's market? Simply put, leaders must quickly evolve into effective thought leaders. Years ago, a conversation among a group of top leaders ensued about the topic of thought leadership. This occurred before thought leadership was among standard vernacular in leadership circles. One leader espoused that a thought leader was one who was paid to think.

By definition, 'A Thought Leader can be recognized as an authority in a specific field, whose expertise is sought and often rewarded, who can be an expert, a historical figure, or a "wise person" with worldly impact.'[4] Practically, these leaders will possess expertise relevant to their field, and the ability to influence others and outcomes that impact their ecosystem. Their ecosystem includes their organization, industry, and others cross functionally (i.e., outside of the particular industry).

Recently, a thought leader engaged a group of top organizational leaders in healthcare. The topics of discussion revolved around the organization's pandemic response, post pandemic organizational operating structure, industry changes, and many others. In short, the team was conducting a series of impact, risk, and planning sessions to find their way out of the storm and into a long-awaited safe haven. The conversation led to a few small studies or organizational assessments.

Surprisingly, the thought leader discovered that the team of top leaders were missing critical elements. Only 20% of the group had a formalized strategic planning process. Also, only 20% of the leaders had a formal change-plan, and none had an organizational knowledge plan. It's important to note that these leaders represented very large business units that served many hundreds of thousands of healthcare customers annually. Without these businesses, care to many critically ill and injured customers would be delayed or unavailable. Thus, suffering or worse would grow unimaginably.

The first thought of the thought leader was, 'How did these leaders and their businesses survive the pandemic and other industry changes over the last few years without these plans?' In reality, the business model was greatly flawed and several key business units were struggling to stay afloat. One bright spot was discovered, related to the 20% group. Those leaders who had strategy and change plans outperformed their peers by 50%. This simply means they met 50% more goals tied to service, quality, and value. Consequently, they fared better during the storm, were more stable, and had a better chance at survival in long term.

The study led to the creation of an operational survival guide of sorts. In short, the enterprise realized its lifeboat needed to be centered around three plans: strategy, change, and knowledge. Let's take a closer look at what the team developed.

The Three Arrows in the Quiver

Strategic Plan- A strategic plan is simply a high-level organizational road map consisting of at least four parts. The purpose of this plan is for top leaders to map out the organization's current market position, where it needs to go, and what attributes are and will be needed for long-term success. The first part of the strategy plan is assessment.

Top leaders must assess the enterprise's market environment from an external lens. The focal points here are market drivers that have, are, and will affect the organization. Also, any gaps that the organization should proactively plan for or address. A micro example would be a community health needs assessment. This information will provide insight for leaders as to what the customer communities around the organization perceive in terms of needs, gaps, and assistance.

The assessment should also consist of an internal review. Leaders must review the organization's performance tied to the basics: service, cost, revenue, quality, and overall value as a starter. Ideally, leaders should review several years, worth of data for favorable or unfavorable trends and patterns. The goal is to determine what is working well versus what needs improvement.

Once the assessment is complete, part two of the strategic plan is crafted. This can be a complicated process, depending upon organizational size, scope, and complexity. Here, attributes such as organizational goals, vision statements, play books, budgets, and other operational aspects of the business are crafted. The goal is to link gaps, goals, and budgets.

The premise is simple. Leaders should exhaustively assess for operational gaps. Then, enterprise goals are set to help fill the identified gaps. Third, budgets are crafted and set to provide resourcing to help meet the organization's goals. The key here is to ensure a linear process is followed. If any of the steps occurs asynchronously, then the organization is likely to not meet goals. Thus, disruption will likely be the next stop along the journey.

Part three and four of the strategy plan are straightforward. These include implementing the strategic plan and reassessing its effectiveness. The implementation phase must be well thought out, organized, and executed precisely. Once implemented, leaders should regularly reassess the plan to ensure its effectiveness. Traditionally, strategy plans were reassessed yearly in healthcare. But, in today's disruptive environment, leaders should reassess their plans more frequently. The thought leader's team decided reassessment would occur, at minimum, monthly, for their survival guide to work effectively.

Change Plan-A change plan is simply a high-level road map to help leaders manage organizational change. The change plan begins at minimum with a few considerations:

- Why are we changing?
- What is success?
- Are there any barriers that would prevent the change from being successful?
- What are the risks to the organization by implementing or not implementing the desired change?
- What's the probability of success?

Leaders should also consider risk-assessing each change before a definitive decision is made. The team used a three-tier risk assessment structure for their change plan. Tier-one risk represented change that was a threat to life, safety, or health. Tier-two change was deemed as critical to mission. Tier-three change represented change that was not a risk to life, safety, health, or the organization's mission. Once assessed, the team categorized each change initiative by its risk, with high-risk change taking priority over lower risk. This helped the organization use its scarce resources wisely and effectively. As with the strategy plan, the leaders reassessed the change plan at least monthly, and made adjustments as needed.

Knowledge Plan-Organizational knowledge simply represents the people who do the work, and the knowledge required to successfully complete tasks so the organization is successful, in long term. The goal is to determine what knowledge exists, current knowledge gaps, and what knowledge will be needed in the future to remain viable. The knowledge plan should include tactics to ensure knowledge is transferred from one person to another, across business units, and outside of the organization. As with the strategy plan, the knowledge plan begins with an assessment.

The assessment should include, at minimum, three tiers. Tier one includes a review of top organizational leaders. There are several considerations at this level. If top leaders vacate their positions, is someone readily available, competent, and trained to fill those roles immediately? If not, a knowledge gap exists. The goal here is to avoid an organizational strategic crisis.

The second knowledge tier relates to divisional leaders. Think of vice presidents or assistant vice presidents in healthcare, who are in charge of divisions comprising several departments. Tier three relates to front-line leaders and workers. This is really where most of the organization's knowledge resides, as this tier is closest to the customer.

Once leaders outline their organization's knowledge structure, they should consider creating a knowledge menu of sorts. In short, the menu constitutes those knowledge focus areas that will determine if the organization survives, can compete, and can win in the current or future market environment. Common menu themes include, but are not limited to: succession planning, cross training, depth in roles, quick guides for completing work, paired work assignments, and the like. The goal here is for leaders to match their knowledge plan menu to the organization's current gaps and future needs. As with the other plans, the leaders decided to set and review various knowledge KPIs (key performance indicators) at least monthly. If unfavorable or unexpected trends or patterns emerged, corrections followed quickly.

Lessons Learned

As the team added the needed arrows to its quiver, there were a few pearls gleaned from the experience that are worth noting. One is that thought leaders should never procrastinate. During the assessment, the thought leader learned that several top leaders were waiting on direction from superiors before crafting their strategy and change plans. The real questions to consider are: Why wait? Can you really afford to wait to plan when the market is constantly changing? What's the collateral damage if your organization is not properly prepared for current and future changes? The realization was that waiting is a form of waste that is detrimental to operational success. Thus, leaders should have a contingency plan in place that can be adjusted if needed.

In addition, the leaders learned that the change and knowledge plans should be folded into the strategic planning process. The key to success was to look forward several years for the strategy plan. In contrast, the focus for the change plan was shorter, with a rolling 12-month view. The knowledge plan was similar to the other plans, but had both shorter and longer foci related to assessment and planning.

Finally, the team learned that each plan should be measured very frequently for success. As with any plan, the million-dollar question to answer is, 'What is success?' The team ensured each plan had measurable KPIs that were reviewed for each plan at minimum monthly. Strategically, the leaders viewed success as goal attainment and improvements tied to service, financials, quality, and overall value. For the change plan, at minimum, the leaders tracked each significant organizational change for successful implementation, as to if it was on time and on budget. For the knowledge plan, the team ensured improvements in basic KPIs such as succession planning, turnover, and cross training were achieved and improved upon.

Summary

The reality is that change is the new norm, the only constant, and will continue for the foreseeable future. If change is planned for properly, then leaders and their organizations will have a better chance for success. If planning and foresight are lacking, change can quickly become disruptive, unhealthy, and dangerous to the enterprise's operating canvas. Thought leaders must ensure their organizations are aware of, prepared for, and actively pursuing change.

In today's world, leadership is no longer affirmed by a title, position, or salary. Leaders are those trusted to guide organizations, customers, and people through turbulent waters from the front. The test of a leader in today's environment is the ability to manage relationships to drive outcomes. Ignorance is no longer bliss and leaders will succeed or fail based on what arrows are in their quiver. The only question is, 'How prepared are you?' A good starting point for all leaders is to ensure they have a well thought out plan for strategy, change, and organizational knowledge.

References

1. Merriam-Webster, 2021. https://www.merriam-webster.com/dictionary/leadership
2. Kauffman Hall, 2020. https://www.kaufmanhall.com/ideas-resources/research-report/2020-mergers-acquisitions-review-covid-19-catalyst-transformation
3. American College of Healthcare Executives (ACHE), 2020. *Hospital CEO Turnover Rate Shows Small Decrease*. https://www.ache.org/about-ache/news-and-awards/news-releases/hospital-ceo-turnover-2020
4. Wikipedia, 2021. https://en.wikipedia.org/wiki/Thought_leader

Leading with Purpose

Leadership & Influence

Leadership can be formally defined as, 'the office or position of a leader.'[1] Does this really espouse what an ideal leader is or should be? Arguably not. Leadership has several components with two frontrunners that are the most noteworthy: science and art.

Leadership science essentially represents technical leadership skills. Traditionally, think of the list of classes taught in business programs to undergraduate or graduate students. Typical topics include, but are not limited to: statistics, organizational theory, strategic planning, finance, accounting, public speaking, and the like. The textbook focus areas are the foundation of the leadership journey, but don't guarantee leadership success.

In contrast, the art of leadership is usually taught in the school of 'hard knocks.' This learning and knowledge is gained by doing, making mistakes in the work environment, and hopefully learning from the hard times to produce better times. As leaders finish formal training programs, they are typically hired or promoted to leadership positions.

Initially, the honeymoon period is laden with visions of grandeur where these new leaders consider their great future salaries, luxurious offices, travel, performance bonuses, recognition, opportunities to lead the masses, and the like. Unfortunately, the honeymoon period never lasts long and reality sets in quickly. The art of leadership really pertains to the ability of true leaders to influence others.

Influence can be defined as, 'The act or power of producing an effect without apparent exertion of force or direct exercise of command.'[2] In layman's terms, leadership is simply influencing others to do what you want them to do, without using force. Influence is manifested in many ways. Leaders who possess high levels of influence tend to exhibit a mixture of hard technical skills, good communication abilities, the ability to garner trust with others, and they can empathize with their counterparts. One of the most important, but often underrated, influencing skills is empathy.

Empathy is simply seeing a situation or perspective through another person's lens. Empathy is developed and nurtured over time through life experiences. It's hard to know what someone else is feeling or sensing without experiencing the same or similar experiences yourself. True leaders will have to master the hard skills and softer skills of leadership in order to lead from the front, achieve sustainable outcomes, and garner the support from others to be successful, in long term.

So, you may be wondering why this topic matters. Is it really relevant and important? The short answer is, more than most know. As we are all adjusting to the post-COVID-19 pandemic operating environment, disruption has become the new norm. The disruption has touched every business and leader type across the globe. Unfortunately, it doesn't appear to be slowing down any time soon.

One great example is the healthcare industry. The traditional way of providing healthcare services has changed forever. One of the most notable trends in this industry has been leadership disruption over the last several years, which has been accelerated by the pandemic. What we once knew, no longer is.

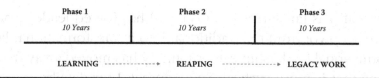

Figure 1.1   Traditional leader career journey phases.

A recent study published by the American College of Healthcare Executives (ACHE) cited, 'The past eight years is the longest period during which hospital CEO turnover rates were 17% or higher since the study began in the early 1980s.'[3] The takeaway is that this leadership disruption is real, not normal variation, and will continue for the foreseeable future. The takeaway is that leaders must lead with purpose in this new operating environment. Unfortunately, many leaders lack the required vision to traverse these everchanging waters, and 'without vision, the people perish' (Proverbs 29:18 KJV).

Traditionally, particularly in healthcare, many leaders followed a three-phase career journey. It's important to note that a leader's career journey is individual-specific, and other pathways exist. See Figure 1.1 for details.

Consider a typical 30-year career, for example. The first ten years typically would be spent learning via education and entry-level leadership experience. Once leaders achieve formal credentials (i.e., degrees, etc.), they are promoted and use their newly acquired skill sets to lead and solve problems. Phase two is typically characterized by the 'reaping' phase. The hard work of learning academically and boots on the ground tends to pay off in this phase. The ideal results would include industry leading outcomes, promotions, higher salaries, and the achievement of major progressive career milestones.

The traditional career phase three is characterized by legacy-building. In this third phase, leaders typically focus on leaving a legacy for the next generation via their accomplishments. Goals would be tied to achieving lasting impacts on the industry's body of knowledge or providing structural resources that would enable the business to succeed well into the future. A good example would be a CEO who builds a new hospital for their health system before retiring. The new facility would serve thousands of customers, staff, and leaders for decades to come. This legacy build would ensure the health system is primed for future success.

The new reality is far different. COVID-19 has forced leaders, particularly in healthcare, to pivot from the traditional into a transformational landscape. The transformational leadership career journey has moved away from a linear model to one that is more cyclical. See Figure 1.2 for details.

Instead of viewing a career over the course of several decades, leaders must now live, work, plan, and achieve with purpose. The key to doing this is vision.

Phase one is the learning phase that never ends. Learning comprises traditional technical skills, but leaders are being forced to learn new hard skills on a regular basis that may be outside their business unit or, in some cases, industry. Think of a nurse leader who has mastered clinical knowledge with a PhD, but now must learn advanced performance improvement methodologies, such as Lean and Six Sigma, in order to improve operational outcomes related to revenues or costs.

The second phase is deploying what is being learned. The key here is being able to leverage knowledge to drive outcomes in real-time. No longer will credentials alone suffice. The plaque on the wall (i.e., degree(s)) has now been replaced with 'What have you done lately' to improve service, cost, and quality of services. The new 'bar' that has been set is doing more with less.

Once leaders learn, deploy the knowledge, and amass reasonable outcomes, they must reassess the market, industry, and customer expectations regularly. If these attributes have shifted, which they do regularly, leaders must pivot their leadership brand, and then re-deploy their skills to drive even more impressive outcomes. The takeaway from this transformational leadership paradigm is that learning, deployment of skills, and outcomes is a continuous fluid process that is evolving rapidly. Moreover, it changes regularly and leaders must evolve to remain relevant.

In years past, change was incremental and leaders could forecast out essentially decades with relative certainty. In today's market, change is rapid, disruptive, and occurs often. Thus, leaders must be agile, learn all the time, plan ahead, and reconfigure their portfolio regularly. Otherwise, the market and subsequent customer expectations will outpace leadership capabilities.

Let's take a closer look at a real example of how leading with purpose paid off.

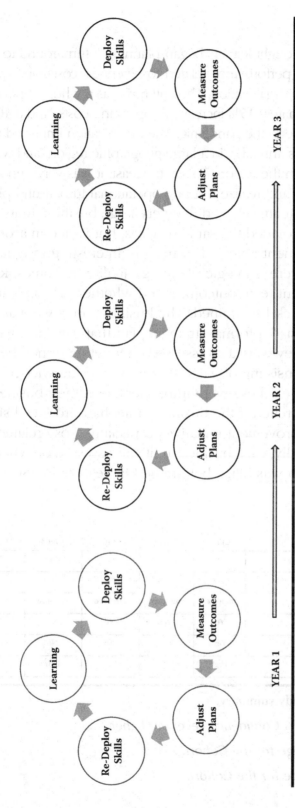

Figure 1.2 Transformational leadership career journey.

Case Study

Recently, a group of thought leaders began planning a turnaround to achieve pre-COVID-19 operational performance related to revenues, costs, and quality of services for a large service organization. The enterprise as a whole experienced a 50% revenue loss, approximately 15% increase in operating costs, and a 10% reduction in quality outcomes due to the pandemic. The organization impacted many tens of thousands of customers annually, in a large geographic region, and was the largest economic contributor in the region. To say the least, it was very important that the team craft, implement, and realize a strong operational turnaround plan quickly.

For the study, the team selected five very large business units as the areas of focus. Each unit provided the same services, but varied in scope, size, and footprint. The assessment revealed some very interesting insights. The focal points of the study were: strategic planning, quality outcomes, knowledge planning, improvement team outcomes, and whether the top leader for each business unit was black belt trained. The business units were assessed as to whether or not they had a formal strategic plan that was hard-wired into the operational fabric. They were also assessed on whether or not the leaders had a knowledge plan consisting of gaps, strengths, and knowledge sharing best practices, and how well these were implemented in their business units. Third, the team researched if the business units had produced significant outcomes tied to improvement initiatives especially those related to service, cost, and quality. Finally, each business unit was assessed on whether or not it had a top leader who was black belt trained in Lean or Six Sigma. See Figure 1.3 for details.

Attribute	Unit 1	Unit 2	Unit 3	Unit 4	Unit 5
Black Belt Leader	Yes	Yes	Yes	No	No
Strategic Plan	Yes	Yes	No	No	No
Quality Outcomes	Improved	Improved	Declined	Declined	Declined
Knowledge Plan	Yes	Yes	No	No	No
Significant Improvement Outcomes	Yes*	Yes*	No	No	No
Overall Performance	High	High	Low	Low	Low

Figure 1.3   Case study summary.

* = Significant at 95% Confidence Level or Higher.

High = Above Average for the Cohort.

Low = Below Average for the Cohort.

The team realized a few findings or themes worth noting. Although the enterprise as a whole struggled with operational metrics such as service and quality, not all business units experienced this trend. Two of the business units (units 1 and 2) were the top performers that continued to thrive in the pandemic and beyond. These units had black belt trained top leaders, a formal strategic plan, a knowledge plan, and they produced significant improvement outcomes related to quality and service.

In contrast, the other three business units did not have formal plans for strategic planning or knowledge sharing. They also did not produce significant outcomes related to improvements in service or quality. Moreover, only one of these units had a black belt trained leader. Thus, each of these business units was low performing and directly contributed to the enterprise's operational declines.

In retrospect, the team learned that those business units led by visionary leaders performed better. The high-performing units had black belt-trained leaders who were forward thinking, skilled in change management, and who regularly deployed their skill sets to improve quality and service. As the market evolved, so did the top-performing business unit leaders. Moreover, these leaders had more knowledge than their counterparts, and leveraged it to produce significant outcomes that were customer-centric. The overarching theme of the study was simple: leaders must lead with purpose, see the big picture, and implement plans that lead to the desired end.

Key Points

- **Purpose**-Leaders must lead with purpose as time is of the essence. The traditional ways of leadership have been and will continue to be disrupted. Leaders must include short-run and long-run visions for the enterprise. The short-run vision should follow a cyclical process, including learning, deploying skills, measuring outcomes, and pivots that adjust to market evolutions regularly. Leadership will not have the luxury of waiting years to see plans come to practice. Successful transformational leaders will need to be able to plan, execute, and achieve desired outcomes quickly. In some instances, the plans may change yearly or sooner, versus the multi-decade plans that have existed in traditional operating environments.

- ■ ***Strategic Plan***-Leaders must create, value, and champion the strategic planning process. Transformational strategic planning must be agile, mirror the current and projected market states, and evolve with time. In the transformational operating environment, strategic planning will include at minimum four phases: gap analysis, planning, execution, and reassessment. In years past, strategic planning focused more on the long run versus short run. As the world adjusts to the post-COVID-19 operating environment, transformational strategic plans will need to be more relevant, flexible, and executable than in years past.
- ■ ***Knowledge Plan***-Organizational knowledge is often one of the most underrated aspects of operations. Often, thought leaders use snazzy tag lines such as knowledge transfer or knowledge sharing for this topic. What do these concepts really mean? The key is for leaders to ensure that their organization's knowledge is documented, captured in a system, and transferred across the enterprise. One easy and practical way to accomplish this is with document management systems and organizational policies.

It seems intuitive, but leaders must never forget that leadership sets culture and culture drives outcomes. The organization's knowledge (i.e., people) represents culture and directly determines if strategic plans succeed or fail. Thus, the most important aspect of leadership is understanding people and their perspectives, and leveraging their knowledge to ensure the enterprise not just survives but thrives in the new transformational market.

Summary

Time is the greatest resource we have been given and we simply don't get a day back once it's gone. A great leader recently said, 'No one has a forever clock.' That statement is truer now than ever. Thus, leaders must lead from the front with purpose, vision, and intent. What once took decades to achieve must now be realized within a fraction of the time. The key takeaway is for leaders to remain agile, champion change, think forward, plan appropriately for current and potential future market requirements, and achieve outcomes. For leaders to succeed in the transformational landscape, they must master strategic planning, knowledge sharing, and improvement methodologies. Simply put, you don't know what you don't measure and you can't improve what you can't see.

References

1. Merriam-Webster, 2021. https://www.merriam-webster.com/dictionary/leadership
2. Merriam-Webster, 2021. https://www.merriam-webster.com/dictionary/influence
3. ACHE, 2021. https://www.ache.org/about-ache/news-and-awards/news-releases/hospital-ceo-turnover-2020

Chapter 2

Risk: The Cardinal Sin of Not Knowing, Assessing, Measuring & Mitigating Risks

Risk Assessing Market Turbulence: Is Disruption at Your Doorstep or a Mile Away?

Market Turbulence

Change is the new normal and only constant. When change levels increase, so does the level of risk to leaders, organizations and their stakeholders. Change occurs when something is made or becomes different.[1] In layman's terms, change is simply a break from the norm or current state. Not all change is bad. But, leaders must be able to discern the difference between normal change or progression and market turbulence.

Turbulence is defined as, 'violent disorder or commotion.'[2] The key here is the nature of this concept. Change can take several forms: slow, incremental or disruptive. Slow change is exactly what as it sounds like. This type of change occurs gradually over time. A close cousin in the change world is incremental change. Incrementally, things tend to change in a step-wise fashion. As time passes, the change is implemented step by step and slowly.

In contrast, change can be disruptive. This is characterized by a radical, sudden and greatly different break from the norm. The adage 'break neck speed' definitely applies here. The key is that turbulent disruptive change is not normal and leaders must handle these transitions wisely. If not planned

DOI: 10.4324/9781003267966-2

for properly, turbulence can quickly put the organization and its leaders in a tailspin. If turbulence results in an operational tailspin, there are only two options: pull out of it or crash and burn.

There are several thoughts to consider in turbulent high-risk environments. Is all change bad? Will change lead to a desired end or disrupt the organization? Is it possible to risk assess markets and organizations to mitigate the impacts of high-risk environments? Does the market signal beforehand that turbulent waters are ahead or is disruption unpredictable? Will all leaders be able to discern between normal progress and market turbulence? We will answer these and other considerations in the following.

For the purpose of this discussion, we will focus on the healthcare industry as an example. For years, this industry was relatively stable and only experienced normal change. Some would call this slow change or expected progress over time. Recently, the healthcare market took on a new nature.

The industry as a whole experienced a few years of tremors related to mounting financial pressures. In short, revenue streams began to decline while costs increased. The only option was to mitigate the risks effectively or die on the vine. Thus, new trends in mergers, acquisitions and hospital closures began to emerge.

Then, the industry started to experience another disruption related to top leaders. See Figure 2.1 for details.[3] The industry for years experienced normal variation in top leader turnover. In the last decade or so (generally speaking), the change took on a turbulent nature. Top leadership disruption increased and did not slow down.

As noted in Figure 2.1, for a seven-year period recently the top leadership turnover remained at record highs for the industry. As noted in the control chart, this is an upward shift evidenced by seven data points in a row above the average line.

In layman's terms, this signal verified something special was happening in the market. Simply put, it was a warning for organizations to take cover, batten down the hatches and steer away from the impending storm. During this time, the industry experienced a 16% increase in CEO turnover when comparing the last two decades. This most definitely was not a routine or normal change. In contrast, top leadership turnover sent the healthcare industry into a tailspin as special cause variation ran ramped. Thus, turbulence ensued and became magnified over time.

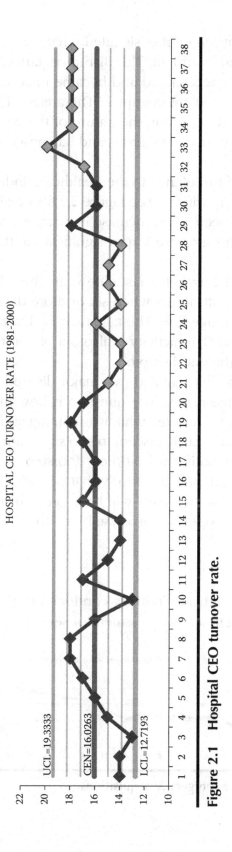

Figure 2.1 Hospital CEO turnover rate.

The takeaway is that the market signaled what was coming. The turbulence did not just appear overnight. This disruptor started small and grew over time. Once prevalent, it accelerated and became uncontrollable quickly. Thus, it qualified as a turbulent disruptor. The adage of 'turning a mole hill into a mountain' applies here. But, the nature of the change was and continues to be highly disruptive, dangerous and has posed catastrophic impacts on the industry.

Another example of turbulence in the healthcare industry relates to the trend in mergers and acquisitions. See Figure 2.2 for details.[4] During the two last decades, there has been a 57% increase in mergers and acquisitions in the healthcare industry. This increase is also significant at the 99% confidence level.

As noted in Figure 2.2, over the last nine years there has been an upward shift in this activity. A shift occurs when six or more data points in a row are above or below the average line. The takeaway is that increases in mergers and acquisitions are real. This activity is also out of control statistically. Thus, it too qualifies as a turbulent disruptor.

In retrospect, the market signaled two major disruptions were brewing long before they became reality. The question is how many leaders and organizations in the industry realized what was coming and prepared? Based on these and other trends, it's easily discernable to say that many failed to discern disruption was a reality until it was at their doorstep.

Let's take a closer look at a case study that provides greater insight to predicting what impact market risks will have on disrupting organizational performance. Is this the operational 'crystal ball' to tell the future? Let's see.

Case Study

As disruption in the healthcare industry continued to rage, a large health system proactively began a risk assessment of several hospitals. The purpose

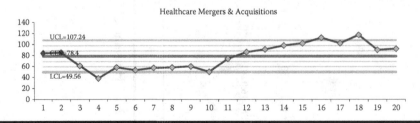

Figure 2.2   Healthcare mergers & acquisitions.

was to identify the degree of risk the market disruptions and subsequent turbulence was having and would have on each facility in the future. The end goal was to identify high-risk areas, pivot, marginalize risks and prevent as much negative impact on the organization as possible.

The tool of choice was a simple risk assessment tool for the market disruption. See Figure 2.3 for details.

The team began by listing each hospital. Then, scored each facility based on several attributes. As noted in the figure, each hospital scored its current cost performance as above, at or below budget. It's important to note that those facilities that scored at or below budget were lower risk.

They also scored each facility in terms of revenue. This attribute was scored similarly to costs. Entities above or at budget for revenues were lower risk than their counterparts. In contrast, hospitals not meeting budget for revenues were high risk.

Third, the scoring efforts focused on turnover for each facility. High turnover was considered to be above 20%. Think of it from a practical perspective. This simply means two out of every ten employees left the enterprise in a specified period of time. Turnover rates of 10%–20% posed average risk while those with less than 10% were low risk.

Next, the team scored each hospital on market trends related to mergers and acquisitions. If the market experiences higher than normal disruption, it was rated as high. If the organizational combinations were at the industry average, then the ranking was medium. Hospitals below the market average received a low ranking for their market.

Finally, each hospital was scored on its goal attainment related to value. The main focal points here were quality and service. In healthcare, the main service metric is typically customer satisfaction scores. The higher the better. For quality, hospitals focus on an array of KPIs (key performance indicators) such as mortality or infection rates for example. Irrespectively, those facilities that met more goals posed less risk to the enterprise and its customers.

Let's take a practical view of the health systems risk findings. The health system risk assessed seven hospitals in its portfolio. All but one was above budget on costs. Also, only two of the facilities were at budget or better for revenues. This is a huge signal of turbulent financial waters. Simply put, the enterprise was high risk for financial insolvency.

For turnover, five of the seven hospitals experienced greater than 20% turnover rates annually. Thus, the majority was high risk in this category.

Hospital	Costs 1-Above Budget 2-At Budget 3-Below Budget	Revenue 1-Below Budget 2-At Budget 3-Above Budget	Turnover 1->20% 2-10% to 20% 3-<10%	Market Mergers & Acquisitions 1-High 2-Medium 3-Low	Goal Attainment 1-<60% 2-60% to 80% 3->80%	Risk Score *Sum Columns 2-6 Lower Score = Higher Risk	Risk Level
Hospital 1	1	1	1	1	1	5	High Risk
Hospital 2	2	1	1	1	2	7	High Risk
Hospital 3	1	1	1	1	1	5	High Risk
Hospital 4	1	1	1	1	1	5	High Risk
Hospital 5	1	1	1	1	2	6	High Risk
Hospital 6	1	3	2	1	1	8	High Risk
Hospital 7	1	2	3	3	1	10	Average

Max Risk 5
Lowest Risk 15
Avg Risk 10

Figure 2.3 Risk assessment tool market disruption.

Persistent and high levels of turnover have been found in many instances to negatively impact cost, quality and service in this industry. Thus, high turnover is very risky.

The team's findings on market mergers and acquisitions revealed all but one hospital was high risk for this activity. In layman's terms, it simply means the market forces were accelerating regionalization of healthcare services. Thus, hospitals were being forced into partnerships for hopeful economies of scale, financial rescues and a chance to survive the storm. This is a consideration for the organization's leaders to quickly assess the need to partner with a stronger organization for survival and a competitive advantage.

The total risk scores and subsequent risk levels were shocking to organizational leaders. In short, all but one hospital was high risk. This simply meant the disruptive and turbulent market waters had a very high probability of impacting the organization. Thus, the failure rate of the health system was extraordinarily high. Practically, disruption was at the organization's door and they had failed to prepare properly.

Summary

As noted, change is the new normal and only constant. Thus, leaders and organizations can predict the future will be different than today. As change evolves and accelerates, risk will continue to grow. The only question is how many leaders will recognize the signals and properly mitigate them before it's too late?

The case study provided great insight into the healthcare industry's turbulent disruption. The key here is that leaders don't know what they don't know. If leaders don't measure risks, it's very likely that turbulent disruptors will be at the organization's doorstep before its realized. The adage 'a day late and a dollar short' applies here.

In retrospect, all change is not bad. Organizations and industries experience normal change over time in revenues, costs, turnover, leadership and the like. The key is knowing when normal change becomes special. This signal is a future predictor that something new or disruptive is on the horizon. Only those leaders with vision and foresight will truly understand, be prepared for and able to avoid disruption in high-risk market environments.

The key is for leaders to use simple tools to risk assess markets and their organizations. Often, ignorance is bliss or so it seems. In reality, ignorance is never bliss. As Hosea (4:6 KJV) wrote, 'My people are destroyed for a lack of knowledge.' Leaders simply don't know what they don't measure.

Today's market, regardless of industry, has changed. The old is gone and the new is here. Effective leaders will be those who know what to measure, when to measure and can discern signals of turbulence a mile away.

References

1. https://dictionary.cambridge.org/us/dictionary/english/change
2. https://www.dictionary.com/browse/turbulence
3. American College of Healthcare Executives (ACHE), 2020. *Hospital CEO Turnover Rate Shows Small Decrease.* https://www.ache.org/about-ache/news-and-awards/news-releases/hospital-ceo-turnover-2020
4. Kauffman Hall, 2020. https://www.kaufmanhall.com/ideas-resources/research-report/2020-mergers-acquisitions-review-covid-19-catalyst-transformation

Risk Assessing Next-Level Roles: Good Fit or a Career Pothole?

Introduction

Merriam-Webster defines promotion as, 'the act or fact of being raised in position or rank' or 'the act of furthering the growth or development of something.' In essence, career promotions are synonymous with vertical movement. Many leaders aspire for more, but is the next level what it's cracked up to be?

Will the next level provide an unending supply of bliss or satisfaction? Is a promotion a sign that someone has finally made it? Once promoted, will this be the ultimate marker of success or are other promotions ahead? Should promotion considerations be risk assessed? Do leaders always know what they think they know? Is perception always reality? Can high-risk situations impede leaders from being successful once promoted? Should leaders or those aspiring be cautious in pursuing next-level roles? Are all roles a good fit or are some career potholes? We will answer these and other considerations in the following.

Often, promotions are glorified due to perks such as enhanced salaries, nice offices, training opportunities, a seat in the room for important decisions and the like. But, to whom much is given, much is required (Luke 12:48).

Promotions are just like a two-sided coin. There are upside and downside risks. The key is to ensure risks of the next-level role do not outweigh the benefits. If so, much consideration is warranted before leaping upward.

This leaves a few thoughts. What about the downside of promotions? Will a promotion require more time commitment than the previous role? Is it a dead-end street or will the new role open new opportunities for the next level? Is the promotion a good fit for the candidate's skills and experience or will they unknowingly be set up for failure from the start? Is the role secure? Is it a requirement for the business to function or just a nice to have a role that could easily be discarded?

The takeaway is that promotions are risky. There are many risks in taking the next role. The role may not be what it was advertised to be. The promotion may require more time away from home, friends, family and personal commitments. Being promoted may provide more money. However, it also comes with more responsibility. This responsibility adds stress, more time at work and a sacrifice of some sort. I learned years ago in an economics class that 'there is no such thing as a free lunch.' In short, everything has a cost.

The question to be answered relates to value. From a leadership perspective, value adds some level of satisfaction, gain or worth to the individual. It essentially makes something or many things better than before. The key is for leaders to ensure the benefits of the next-level role outweigh the costs. If not, the next step will be in a career pothole instead of a good fit.

Recently, a rising leader looked over the hedges into another organization and said, 'I would love have a leadership role like that.' The role was over a large business unit. It required 24/7 oversight of hundreds of personnel. The salary was very competitive and the title provided some level of prominence.

A colleague overheard the comment, engaged the leader and advised caution. The conversation shifted to a new direction not considered. A simple question was posed, 'Have you considered the risk of taking that role?' The leader in question paused with a blank stare. The adage 'deer in the headlights' or 'what sparkles doesn't always shine' applies here.

The next step was the creation of a simple risk assessment tool. See Figure 2.4 for details.

The risk tool focused on several attributes that were ranked on respective levels of risk. These attributes include compensation, fit with current skills/education, promotion potential, quality of life, time requirements and role security. To summarize, the risk tool helps candidates considering promotions determine the likelihood that they will succeed, be paid a competitive wage,

Role	Role Compensation 1-Below Market 2-At Market 3-Above Market	Fit with Skills/Education 1-No 2-Yes	Promotion Potential 1-No Potential 2-Some Potential 3-High Potential	Quality of Life 1-High Stress 2-Average Stress 3-Low Stress	Time Requirement 1->50 Hours Per Week 2-40 to 50 Hours Per Week 3-40 Hours Per Week	Required Organizational Role? 1-No 2-Yes	Risk Score *Sum Column 2-7 Lower Score = Higher Risk	Risk Level
Role 1	1	1	1	1	1	1	6	High Risk
Role 2	2	2	2	1	2	2	11	Average
Role 3	3	2	3	2	3	2	15	Low

Avg Score / Risk Level:

	Role Compensation	Fit with Skills/Education	Promotion Potential	Quality of Life	Time Requirement	Required Organizational Role?
Avg Score	2.0	1.7	2.0	1.3	2.0	1.7
Risk Level	High Risk	High Risk	High Risk	High Risk	High Risk	High Risk

Max Risk 6
Lowest Risk 16
Avg Risk 11

Figure 2.4 Risk assessment tool.

have future opportunities if they take the role and have a reasonably good quality of life. The key here is projecting risk for each attribute.

Let's use a practical example of the scenario previously noted. The leader was a top performer and felt the next level was deserved, a viable option and the next career step. This leader compared three open leadership roles on the risk attributes previously noted. The goal was to find the best fit that posed the least amount of risk to success, quality of life and future potential. The outcomes were surprising.

As noted in Figure 2.4, the first role was the leadership position responsible for running the large business unit. When each attribute was risk scored, the role overall was high risk. In short, the pay was less than expected, the fit with the leader's skills was low, the time commitment was high and the future potential of using the role as a catapult to the next level was very low. Moreover, this role was not a required element for the business to function. If operations declined, it would be the first on the chopping block. Thus, the position was very high risk for this candidate. As previously noted, what sparkles does not always shine.

In contrast, the leader scored two other potential roles. Role 2 only posed an average risk to the leadership candidate. The main concern here was limited quality of life due to enhanced stress levels of the job and more time commitment above the normal 40-hour work week. Also, the role had an average promotion potential. Thus, the leader knew a lot of work was ahead in order to get to the next level. The adage 'nothing comes easy' applies here.

The leader also scored one last role. Role 3 scored the best as low risk. This role's pay, quality of life, security and promotion potential was ideal. Thus, it was the least risky next-level role for this candidate. The adage of 'path of least resistance' applies here as the value far exceeded its risk potential. This role would require the least amount of stress and work for the next level.

The leader also analyzed all three roles per attribute. When viewing each attribute in Figure 2.4 vertically, they were all high risk on average. This simply means that any of the attributes for the group of next-level positions could be hazardous to the candidate if not mitigated properly. Simply put, it's worth the time and effort to consider other attributes outside of compensation when looking for the next-level role. In addition to money, other attributes are just as important to ensure success. Job likeability, quality of life, role security and others matter. The adage of 'money cannot buy happiness' applies here. The key is knowing the risk of each attribute.

Summary

In review, the case study provides great insight into risk assessing promotion opportunities. As the leader learned, we must be careful what we ask for. Often, perception is not always reality. Also, what sparkles does not always shine. The key is to find the diamond in the rough that presents the least amount of risk.

In reality, promotions bring risk. Risk is not always bad, but high-risk levels can be harmful to next-level promotion candidates if not mitigated properly. Looking back, leadership can be a very rewarding and challenging venture. But, for those who don't risk assess the journey ahead the next level may not be what it's cracked up to be.

Promotion is not always a sign that someone has finally made it. Often, those who choose the next role with caution or avoid high-risk roles are wiser than their counterparts who move ahead without consideration for risk. The ultimate marker of success relates to those leaders who find roles that fit them best, provide infinite levels of satisfaction and afford the opportunity to help others at every turn. It has been said if one finds their purpose, they will never work a day in their life. In contrast, stepping into the wrong role for the wrong reasons can lead to a valueless experience.

The key is for leaders to risk assess next-level roles. Often, even the most experienced leaders don't always know what they think they know. Risk is a liability that must be measured, analyzed and mitigated at every turn. Otherwise, leaders or those aspiring to be won't find the right fit. In reality, the next career step will be a pothole.

Risk Assessing Organizational Training & Knowledge Capabilities: Is It a Knowledge Expander or a Waste of Resources?

Introduction

Is it possible to risk assess organizational training? Is all training and knowledge transfer a value add or just training for the sake of training? Should leaders be able to volunteer for knowledge opportunities or is it better for it to be required? Is it possible to risk assess organizational knowledge to find pearls and pitfalls? Is organizational knowledge a risky business or just business as usual? When scarcity of resources is present, how will leaders determine which knowledge is the greatest value and lowest risk? We will answer these and other considerations in the following.

Knowledge transfer is exactly what it sounds. Simply put, this concept occurs when skills and knowledge are transferred across the enterprise and beyond. There are several organizational levels to consider. The macro view is how knowledge transfers from one division or entity to the next. The meso view is when knowledge transfer occurs from department to department. The micro view is how knowledge transfers from one person to another. There is also an external factor. This external knowledge transfer occurs when the organization shares knowledge to outside stakeholders across the industry and beyond. Publications, presentations and the like serve these functions.

Irrespectively, organizational knowledge is very important and training is one important aspect of ensuring a successful transfer. Recently, a large service organization considered its knowledge transfer strategic plan for the next few years. The realization was that finances were tight and the projection for this trend tends to continue. Thus, leaders were forced to ration training resources across the enterprise.

This was a juggling act to say the least. On the one hand, the leaders had to ensure the organization had adequate knowledge to compete and grow its service area. On the other hand, resources were limited and some knowledge transfer activities were not feasible. In short, the enterprise had great knowledge goals and a 'shoe string' budget to make the plan a reality.

Let's take a closer look. The enterprise leaders had several decisions to make in rationing resources. Figure 2.5 outlines a micro example with great organizational impact. They used a simple risk assessment tool focusing on training. The team listed a few training focus areas presented by organizational leaders.

Next, they scored each training option on several attributes. These factors included: benefit potential, risk level, whether the training was required for the organization's work and was it already budgeted or an additional expense. As noted in Figure 2.5, there were three enterprise knowledge decisions that needed direction.

One, enterprise leaders needed improvements in quality, service and cost. So, they considered training nearly one thousand leaders and staff in improvement methodologies such as Lean and Six Sigma. The organization spend would be several hundred thousand dollars just to complete the basic training enterprise wide. The hope was to realize a 1:10 return ratio. Simply put, for every dollar spent on training the organization would see a ten-dollar return.

Training Focus	Benefit Potential 1-Immediate Benefit to Life, Safety, Health 2-Immediate Benefit to Mission 3-Important, but not an immediate Benefit to 1 or 2	Risk Level 1-Risk to Life, Safety, Health 2-Risk to Mission 3-Important, but not a risk to 1 or 2	Required for the Organizational Role? 1-No 2-Yes	Is it Budgeted? 1-No 2-Yes	Risk Score *Sum Columns 2-5 Lower Score = Higher Risk	Risk Level
Lean Green Belt	1	1	1	1	4	High Risk
Analytics Certification	2	2	2	1	7	Average
PhD Offering	3	3	2	1	9	Low

Avg Score 2.0 2.0 1.7 1.0
Risk Level High Risk High Risk High Risk High Risk

Max Risk 4
Lowest Risk 10
Avg Risk 7

Figure 2.5 Training risk assessment tool.

Two, the leaders contemplated providing funding for several thought leaders to attain advanced analytics certifications. The industry was demanding strong analytics programs and this was an identified opportunity during strategic planning sessions. The cost was minimal and the expected return was insight by leveraging these data to paint a broader picture of the organization's performance, risks and opportunities to improve. These returns were expected to improve revenue and cost streams. Thus, assist in maximizing profitability.

The third knowledge consideration related to a top-performing thought leader's proposal. The leader made an offer to the organization's top leader. The proposal was simple. If the organization supported and funded the leaders PhD program, then the leader would make a time and return on investment commitment to the organization. The cost for funding the advanced degree was over $90,000 and the return was to be determined at a later date.

When using Figure 2.5, the team realized that the Lean green belt training for several hundred leaders and staff was high risk. The benefit of this training would provide a direct improvement to life, safety and health. Moreover, the risk of this knowledge not being incorporated into the organizations operating fabric would directly impede services to humanity. Thus, jeopardize safety and effectiveness of services. This training option was not required and was not budgeted.

As noted in Figure 2.5, the analytics certification for a few thought leaders was average risk. The benefit of this training would ensure the organization could continue to meet its mission to stakeholders. The risk level was also a risk to the mission if the training was not included in the strategic plan. The plan was to require this certification for certain roles and it too was not in the budget. Thus, this expenditure would have to be an exception.

Finally, the team risk scored the PhD proposal. This knowledge option was scored as low risk. Simply put, this knowledge was important to the enterprise. But, it was not a direct benefit or risk to life, health, safety or mission. Moreover, the goal was to make it mandatory for a certain role. It also was not in the budget.

After scoring the knowledge requests, the team decided to focus on the highest risk areas first. Then, table the lowest risk training foci for another time when resources were more plentiful. As a result, the funding for knowledge transfer went to Lean green belt training. The organization realized a 1:3 ratio of return. There were significant improvements from this training, but more opportunities still existed to achieve the total expected return.

So, what did we learn? Often, the flashy aspects of organizational knowledge get the funding when scarcity exists. But, the enterprise in the previous example used risk scores to assist in making more practical funding decisions. The reality was that the best choice was made for the customer base.

The enterprise subsequently focused on the basics which directly impacted many thousands of customers positively. Moreover, the organization realized a significant return. The moral of the story is that risk is often a good truth serum for organizational decisions. As noted, the risk assessment tool helped filter out the flashy from what was really needed.

Once funding was secured, the organization implemented yet another level of rationing. Out of thousands of leaders and staff, only a small portion could receive the training due to the scarcity of funding. Figure 2.6 is a simple rationing tool the organization used. It too is a risk scoring system of a similar form.

The leaders scored each work area on several attributes: organizational need, whether the training was required for the specific role, if the leader or staff member volunteered for the training and seniority was used as the tie breaker if needed. In short, the organization allowed those working in high need operational areas in which the training was a role requirement to be trained first. Again, the highest risk areas should be mitigated first.

Those who volunteered first and met the other requirements were granted access to training in the initial cohort. Once the cohort structure was fully implemented, other staff and leaders in less risky areas were entered into the program as noted in Figure 2.6. The rollout and training plan was very successful. The organization found this to be a judicious, fair and risk-centered approach to transferring organizational knowledge. It's important to note that this is simply an example of rationing training resources in a scarce environment. Organizational leaders must ensure their training plans follow their organizational and regulatory requirements in administering knowledge sharing.

Summary

The key is that change is the new norm and only constant. The greater the change, the greater the risk. Thus, enterprise leaders must counterbalance risk with knowledge. But, in market environments where resources are scarce how will leaders determine which attributes of knowledge are the least risky and add the most value. The sure bet is a risk assessment tool.

Training Focus	Organizational Need Per Area 1-High 2-Medium 3-Low	Required for the Organizational Role? 1-Yes 2-No	Leader Interest 1-Volunteer 2-Required	Seniority 1-High 2-Medium 3-Low	Risk Score *Sum Columns 2-5 Lower Score = Higher Priority	Priority Level
Lean Green Belt Cohort 1	1	1	1	1	4	High
Lean Green Belt Cohort 2	2	2	2	1	7	Average
Lean Green Belt Cohort 3	2	2	2	2	8	Low
Avg Score		1.7	1.7	1.3		
Risk Level	High Risk	High Risk	High Risk	High Risk		

Max Risk 4
Lowest Risk 10
Avg Score 7

Figure 2.6 Rationing training tool.

In summary, the study reveals that it is possible to risk assess organizational training and knowledge sharing. Also, all training and knowledge transfer don't add the same level of value add. Thus, some knowledge sharing options may be training for the sake of training or of less value to the customer. Therefore, it's imperative for thought leaders to identify, assess, analyze and prioritize organizational risks as it related to knowledge.

Otherwise, leaders may never find the knowledge pearls and subsequently only stumble into training pitfalls. The key is that organizational knowledge is a risky business and can never be viewed as just business as usual. Organizations and their leaders don't know what they don't measure. Ignorance is never bliss. Thus, leaders must be wise in how they prioritize, fund and share organizational knowledge. Otherwise, training efforts will be like throwing darts at a dart board in a dark room. Leaders will always be off target.

Risk Assessing Flight Risks: Predicting Leadership Turnover with Risk Tools

The Impact of Turnover

Is it possible to predict leadership turnover? Is turnover a destructive force on organizations or just normal change? Is all turnover bad or a mechanism to refresh organizational leadership ranks over time? Will turnover affect organizational bottom lines if not curtailed? Can organizations survive with persistent, chronic and high levels of leadership turnover long-term? Can simple risk assessment tools help leaders understand the actual and potential effect of turnover on the enterprise? Will proactive risk assessments help organizational leaders mitigate high flight risks to ensure organizational stability? We will answer these and other considerations in the following.

Turnover is one of the most disruptive forces organizations face. Per Wikipedia, turnover is defined as the 'relative rate at which an employer gains and loses staff.' It's comparable to adding water to a vehicle's gas tank. The vehicle will run for a short while. But, eventually the engine will fail and leave the passengers sitting on the side of the road.

Often, leaders and their organizations overlook or underestimate the impact of turnover. Generally speaking, there are two basic types of turnover: normal and disruptive. Normal or expected turnover occurs over time. This is to be expected and more times than not occurs in a controlled fashion.

Common examples of normal turnover are retirements, life circumstances that require leaders to relocate geographically due to family needs and education. Over time, leaders may upskill and receive advanced education that affords other vertical opportunities. Thus, turnover results.

In contrast, turnover can be very toxic and dangerous. This type of turnover is disruptive as it many times creates unstable operating environments that must be corrected quickly. Disruptive turnover can be characterized as being chronic, recurring, consistent and higher than the market or industry average. The key here is that it creates organizational turbulence that is unhealthy.

The takeaway is that turnover is needed in some instances, but can quickly become unmanageable and eventually sink the organizational ship if not mitigated. Think of forest management. Annually, forest rangers in various parts of the US conduct controlled burns in various forests. The key word here is 'controlled.' The purpose is to burn away old or dead foliage that is harmful to the forest's growth. This controlled activity is helpful, adds value and will produce new growth.

In contrast, when these forest fires get out of control they grow quickly, irradicably and are very destructive. Often, controlled fires can turn into wild fires. The key word here is 'wild.' The nature of the problem is 'wild,' out of control and unpredictable. Unfortunately, if not curtailed quickly, these wild fires damage life, safety, property and health of many unintended customers. Simply put, the end goal is to keep turnover under control.

Case Study

Let's take a look at a practical example in healthcare. For several years, a large health system was experiencing higher than normal top leadership turnover. Historically, top leaders worked for the organization their entire lives in most instances. These appointments were highly prized and vacancies were rare. Double-digit seniority was the norm.

Due to normal attrition, the top leader role in the enterprise became vacant and a new leader was hired in from the outside. Shortly after, the turnover churn began. The new top leader began to implement a series of leadership transitions. The entire top leadership team was replaced quickly. This is comparable to the controlled burn example previously noted. The intent was to create new organizational growth with an injection of fresh talent, perspectives and experience.

Unfortunately, the turnover did not stop with the first round of new leadership appointments. The wild fire example applies here. The new appointees lasted at best two years on average and the situation quickly became out of control. The organization went from near-zero top leadership turnover rates to nearly 30% annually which far exceeded the market rate for the industry.

See Figure 2.7 for details. During this time, the industry average for top leadership turnover was 16%. The healthcare industry as a whole was experiencing a seismic shift. However, the health system of focus shifted from a stable operating environment to a crisis mode quickly.

You may be wondering why this matters? Was the change and chaos significant? Is it really worth mentioning? In short, the decision to clean sweep the top leadership team was the fire starter. The turnover had disastrous effects on service, financials and quality of services. These downturns were not just an infection point. They became the new trend and grew over time. The adage of turning 'a mole hill into a mountain' is applied here. Another cliché that is applicable would be the snowball effect.

In retrospect, the organization's top leadership churn began a wild fire that raged for several years. Financially, the turnover and its subsequent operational instability cost the enterprise hundreds of millions of dollars in financial loss. Moreover, quality and customer satisfaction rates plummeted. During the period, operational goal attainment dropped by over 30%. The takeaway is that the situation was untenable and not sustainable.

So, was this situation avoidable? Could the enterprise leaders have predicted that leaders would cycle in and out of the organization at an unhealthy rate? Let's take a closer look at a simple risk assessment tool for flight risks.

Risk Assessing High Flight Risks

The organization learned from its past challenges and created a risk assessment tool to determine the flight risk level of leadership roles. See Figure 2.8 for details.

Step one, the team identified leadership roles of interest. Then, scored each role on several attributes as noted in the figure. The first couple focal points related to the current market position. Was market demand and supply for each role high or low? The worst-case scenario was for high market demand and low market supply.

The next attribute relates to turnover rates for the role. The scale of measure used was >20%, 10%–20% and <10%. The goal here is for each role to have less turnover. But, higher risk was associated with a higher turnover percentage.

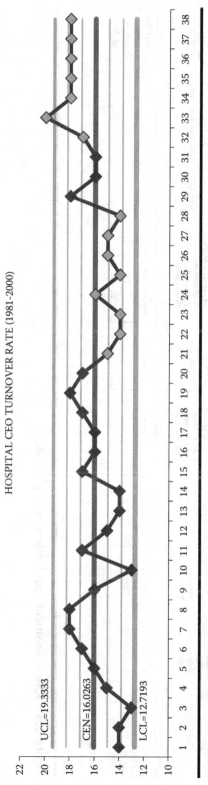

Figure 2.7 Hospital CEO turnover rate (1).

Leader	Market Demand for the Role 1-High 2-Medium 3-Low	Market Supply for the Role 1-Low 2-Medium 3-High	Role Turnover 1->20% 2-10% to 20% 3-<10%	Organizational Compensation for the Role 1-Below Market 2-At Market 3-Above Market	Internal Vertical Opportunities 1-Low 2-Medium 3-High	Current Leader Skill/Education Level 1-Exceeds Role Requirements 2-Meets Role Requirements	Operational Outcomes 1-High 2-Medium 3-Low	Risk Score *Sum Columns 2-8 Lower Score=Higher Risk	Flight Risk Level
Leader 1	3	3	3	3	3	2	3	20	Ideal
Leader 2	2	1	3	2	2	1	1	12	High Risk
Leader 3	1	1	3	2	2	2	3	14	Average
Leader 4	1	2	1	1	1	2	2	10	High Risk
Leader 5	1	1	3	1	2	1	1	10	High Risk

Max Risk 7
Lowest Risk 20
Avg Risk 14

Figure 2.8 Risk assessment tool leadership flight risk.

Organizational compensation was also used as an indicator of flight risk. The scoring matrix here was: above market, below market and at market. Those roles that were paid below market are the highest risk. Obviously, if leaders can make more money for the same job elsewhere, there is a greater chance of turnover.

The next three attributes relate to the promotion opportunities, current leader credentials and operational outcomes. The organization owned the promotion attribute. Were there adequate vertical movement options for higher performers? The ideal answer is yes. But, reality is that this is not always the case. Low opportunity levels for top talent are higher risk for flight.

In terms of credentials and outcomes, the highest risk leaders were those whose credentials exceeded the basic requirements for the role. Simply put, they had more potential to do more than the current role needed. Also, top talent leaders were those who produced higher levels of operational goals. This was measured in goal attainments for KPIs related to service, cost, quality and the like. Essentially, anything that added value to the customer.

Once each attribute was rated for each leader, the tool provides a risk score. Lower scores equate to higher risk. Then, the tool applies a flight risk level. High flight risk leaders are those who scored above average as noted in Figure 2.8.

Let's take a practical look at the risk assessment tool. The organization chose five top leaders for the assessment initially. This was the baseline. Market demand was high for 60% of these leaders. In comparison, market supply was also high for 60% of the roles. This simply meant these roles were important, if interest across the industry and scarce (i.e., not a dime a dozen).

In contrast, these roles had very little turnover on average. Only 20% of the leadership roles in the pilot has 20% turnover or higher. Simply put, most of the leaders valued tenure and tended to stay longer. The goal here is less turnover, obviously.

Forty percent of the roles were high risk for organizational compensation. This subgroup was being paid below market which is a concern. Moreover, 80% of the leaders occupying these roles have average or greater opportunities for vertical promotions. This is a good score overall.

Of the subgroup, 40% had more talent than was required for their respective roles. Also, 40% of the leaders performed above their peers. These attributes separate the 'pros' from the 'joes.' On a serious note, this 40% subgroup represented those who were the highest risk of flight. They performed well, had great credentials and were highly prized. Thus, a focal point for mitigating flight risks.

When the subgroup was scored globally, 60% of the leaders were high risk for leaving the organization. Moreover, 20% were average risk of leaving. The interpretation of the risk assessment is simple. The organization has work to do quickly. If 60% of the leaders who are top talent leave, this will result in turbulence the enterprise cannot afford. Turbulence will impact service, cost, quality and subsequently each customer. Thus, mitigation and prevention efforts were a high priority.

Proactive Solutions to Turnover Risks

Anytime high-risk levels exist, leaders must address them quickly. Based on the case study, here are a few simple solutions to mitigate the flight risks. One, leaders should spend time with each leader in the study. The adage of being quick to listen and slow to speak applies here (James 1:19). The intent is to learn what each leader values, wants and sees as success (career wise). Then, co-create a road map to help the leader achieve and see progress in their careers. Doing something is definitely better than doing nothing. The end goal is to find the next role for the top talent leaders.

Two, the enterprise should conduct a market assessment related to compensation. If possible, those leaders below market on salaries should be addressed first. The key is to remove any financial incentive that may exist for leaving the organization. The adage 'you get what you pay for' applies here.

Three, leaders should explore training options for the leaders in the assessment. Resource dependent, this is a relatively quick and sometimes reasonably cost-effective way to retain top talent. Training could take many forms such as certification classes, advanced degrees, cross training in areas outside of the leader's comfort zone, paired assignments with senior leaders, stretch assignments and the like. The goal here is to grow the leader regardless if a promotion is readily available or not. This investment can go along way with top talent.

Finally, another option relates to work life. Do the leaders prefer remote work, onsite work or a combination of the two? If possible, allowing autonomy in how work gets done is typically a relatively cost-effective and higher satisfying (from the leader's perspective) solution. Obviously, this option is organization and role dependent. However, allowing leaders to co-create their work space can be a great value add.

Summary

In today's world, change is the only constant and new normal. Change takes on many forms, but the goal for enterprise leaders is to control changes that impact the organization as much as possible. As we learned from the case study, a byproduct of change is risk. Moreover, leaders don't know what they don't measure.

Ignorance is never bliss. Thus, leaders must know, analyze and respond appropriately to risk. Otherwise, the controlled fire will become a wild fire quickly. The key to risk is seeing the forest for the trees. The market and organizations individually are living beings, so to speak. Thus, they constantly send signals of their direction, next pivot and potential risks.

The takeaway is that it is possible to predict leadership turnover and flight risks. Turnover is both a normal expectation and a destructive force on organizations if not controlled. If the controlled turnover fire evolves into a turbulent wild fire, organizational bottom lines and their customers will be highly affected and disrupted. In reality, many organizations will struggle to survive with persistent, chronic and high levels of leadership turnover long-term.

Thus, a simple risk assessment tool is worth its weight in gold for helping leaders understand the actual and potential effects of high flight risks. Those who notice the risk signals early and respond quickly will have the greatest chance of controlling the disruptor. In contrast, those organizations that are proactive and assume versus actually know their risks will quickly become the next case study.

In summary, risk does matter. Leadership turnover is a big deal. Risk assessments for leadership flight risks add value at every turn. The key is to look forward, measure, analyze and respond proactively to high flight risks. Otherwise, disruption is just around the corner.

Reference

American College of Healthcare Executives (ACHE), 2020. *Hospital CEO Turnover Rate Shows Small Decrease.* https://www.ache.org/about-ache/news-and-awards/news-releases/hospital-ceo-turnover-2020

Assessing Risk for Partnerships: Run for the Hills or Welcome to the Family?

Introduction

Are all partnerships a good fit? Does risk play a role in the success or failure of organizational mergers, acquisitions and the like? Is risk a relationship disruptor or just normal current? Is it possible for leaders to risk assess potential partnerships and predict the success potential of coming together? Do leaders really know what they know or is a risk assessment warranted? Are corporate partnerships risky business or just business as usual? We will answer these and other considerations in the following.

Merriam-Webster defines a partnership as, 'a relationship resembling a legal partnership and usually involving close cooperation between parties having specified and joint rights and responsibilities.' There are many types of corporate partnerships. But, the main focal points tend to be control, resourcing and benefits of coming together. Mergers and acquisitions tend to be risky business due to a variety of factors. Failure rates for these combinations can be as high as 70%–90%.[1] The million-dollar question literally is why?

Partnerships can take many forms from simple joint ventures to acquisitions and everything in between. See Figure 2.9 for a simple schematic.

With joint ventures, for example, the premise is shared control by the two parties. The hope is for the venture to produce better outcomes as a combined organization. Acquisitions on the other hand essentially occur when one organization buys another. Thus, retaining control and holding majority rights to resourcing, decisions and achieved benefits from the combination. The concept of sharing is replaced with majority control.

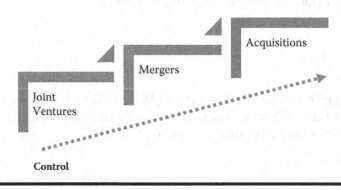

Figure 2.9 Partnership schematic.

Regardless of type, all partnerships have a desired end of some sort. For some, the end goal may be growth in service area, higher revenues, cost savings and the like. For others, the benefits of coming together may include access to capital dollars, advanced technology, improved quality of services and other strategic delivery service models. Regardless, success is determined by how much better the new organization is post combination versus pre-partnership. If the risks outweigh the benefits, then caution is warranted.

This leads to an interesting question. How will leaders know how risky partnerships are if they do not measure risk? Moreover, if risk is not assessed and analyzed, how will organizations know whether to run for the hills or welcome the new partner into the enterprise's family? The key here is leaders don't know what they don't measure.

Example 1

Let's take a look at a healthcare example for context. Recently, two large organizations began negotiations for merging two large business units. Both units impacted hundreds of thousands of customers annually and had large regional operational foot prints. The leaders on both sides took a shotgun approach for the combination with very little forethought. The financial impact of merging both business units was tens of millions of dollars annually.

The initial thought and perspective of the two organizations was that these are like business units in every way. Thus, the similarities should make for a smooth transition. The key is the leaders on both sides 'thought' instead of measuring for objective evidence. Also, risk was not a part of the conversation. The adage of ignorance is bliss applies here.

In short, the initial goal was an equal partnership of shared control, costs and benefits. However, the leaders failed many times to bring the two business units together formally. Each time the teams began to combine the operations, a roadblock of some sort arose. After spending months of time and millions of dollars on the process, the leaders on both sides realized the cultures were so far apart that the combination was not going to be successful.

From a distance, the two parties appeared to be very similar. The partnership appeared to be a diamond in the rough. However, in reality it turned out to be thorn in the leadership cadre's side that simply would not go away. Simply put, the leaders did not know what they thought they knew. Moreover, perception was not reality.

After a long journey, the two sides ended negotiations. They went their separate ways operationally speaking. The deal was a huge failure, waste of time and loss of millions of dollars. Most importantly, the process tarnished the local reputations of both parties. So, was it worth it? The short answer is no.

In retrospect, a team was assembled for an after-action review. The goal was to unveil the risks to both enterprises for the partnership and determine why efforts failed. The adage a day late and a dollar short applies here. Irrespectively, a simple risk assessment tool was created for the analysis. See Figure 2.10 for details.

The team studied nine attributes including profitability, organizational operational goal attainment (service, cost and quality), growth potential, cash reserves, market disruption potential, benefit potential, risk level, cultural alignment and strategic planning. These attributes allowed the organization to view the risks to all parties in a simple showcase. The key was to display the likelihood of the combined organization's success in operations, finances and service delivery.

When reviewing Figure 2.10, the risk tool screams high risk. Seventy-eight percent of the attributes were high risk for failure. Only operational goal attainment and strategic planning were low-risk indicators. Of the two business units, one was low risk and the other high risk. Was the probability of the perceived partnership's success the same as a coin toss? Short answer, not far off.

The takeaway from the after-action review is as follows:

- Finances were at high risk of not being readily available or exhausted quickly post combination.
- The market was a high-risk proposition as turbulence was creating higher than normal incentives for organizations to partner.
- The risks and benefits of the partnership both directly impacted life, safety and health of many hundreds of thousands of customers. Does the phrase 'high-risk poker' resonate here?
- Cultural alignment did not exist. The cultures were so different that the partnership was doomed for failure before it began.

So, what did we learn in retrospect? One, perception was not reality. Both organizations leaders perceived great likeness which simply did not exist.

Organization	Profitability 1-Not Profitable 2-At Breakeven 3-Profitable	Organizational Goal Attainment 1-<70% 2-70% to 80% 3->80%	Growth Potential 1-No Growth 2-Some Growth 3-High Growth	Cash Reserves 1-< 100 Days 2-100 to 200 Days 3->200 Days	Market Disruption Potential 1-High 2-Medium 3-Low	Benefit Potential 1-Immediate Benefit to Life, Safety, Health 2-Immediate Benefit to Mission 3-Important, but not an immediate Benefit to 1 or 2	Risk Level 1-Risk to Life, Safety, Health 2-Risk to Mission 3-Important, but not a risk to 1 or 2	Cultural Alignment 1-Different Cultures 2-Similar Cultures 3-Same Cultures	Organizational Strategic Planning 1-No Plan 2-Basic Plan 3-Advanced Plan	Risk Score *Sum Columns 2-10 Lower Score = Higher Risk	Risk Level
Organization 1	1	2	2	1	1	1	1	1	2	12	High Risk
Organization 2	3	3	2	2	3	1	1	1	3	19	Low
Avg Score	2.0	2.5	2.0	1.5	2.0	1.0	1.0	1.0	2.5		
Risk Level	High Risk	Low Risk	High Risk	High Risk	High Risk	High Risk	High Risk	High Risk	Low Risk		

Max Risk 9
Lowest Risk 27
Avg Risk 18

Figure 2.10 Risk assessment tool.

One unit was high risk and the other low risk. Ideally, both partners should be low risk to achieve maximum success.

Two, risks were never assessed during or before negotiations. The leaders took a lot for granted and assumed the perceptions of likeness would override the unforeseen reality of great differences. A different lens and risk tool were greatly needed. In retrospect, the tool shows that the proposed coming together was all but ensured an undesired end.

Finally, proper measurement and analysis would have saved both parties a lot of time, resources and money. Ignorance is never bliss. What leaders don't know can hurt them and the organizations they serve. The right perspective is data driven with evidence-based decision-making following.

Example 2

Let's look at another example from a different lens. Recently, a leader of a very large service organization announced their growth plans. The plan included the acquisition of five competitors. The deals are worth billions of dollars and impact millions of customers annually. Thus, this growth strategy is perceived to be high risk by nature.

Looking forward using the risk tool in Figure 2.11, a simple question remains unanswered. What's the risk to these growth efforts? If we assess the five acquisitions on the same attributes, the projected risk is surprising. All nine attributes for combining these five businesses are high risk. From current financials to organizational cultures, the risk is excessive.

Also, 60% of the individual businesses are high risk as noted in Figure 2.11. In contrast, only 20% of the units are low risk. The key here is the goal of the acquisitions is to increase the enterprise footprint, increase profitability, realize efficiencies and enhance services. If all these have a very high risk of failure, will the end justify the means? Moreover, will these combinations add value or just use the organization's resources more quickly?

The reality is that time will tell. However, it would be prudent for these leaders to formally consider the risks these growth strategies pose. The worst-case scenario would be for the risk to outweigh the reward. Thus, the acquisitions result in a family feud, organizationally speaking.

Summary

In today's world, change is the only normal and constant. With high change environments, uncertainty looms. In uncertainty, risk grows and can quickly

Organization	Profitability 1-Not Profitable 2-At Breakeven 3-Profitable	Organizational Goal Attainment 1-<70% 2-70% to 80% 3->80%	Growth Potential 1-No Growth 2-Some Growth 3-High Growth	Cash Reserves 1-<100 Days 2-100 to 200 Days 3->200 Days	Market Disruption Potential 1-High 2-Medium 3-Low	Benefit Potential 1-Immediate Benefit to Life, Safety, Health 2-Immediate Benefit to Mission 3-Important, but not an immediate Benefit to 1 or 2	Risk Level 1-Risk to Life, Safety, Health 2-Risk to Mission 3-Important, but not a risk to 1 or 2	Cultural Alignment 1-Different Cultures 2-Similar Cultures 3-Same Cultures	Organizational Strategic Planning 1-No Plan 2-Basic Plan 3-Advanced Plan	Risk Score *Sum Columns 2-10 Lower Score = Higher Risk	Risk Level
Organization 1	1	1	1	1	1	1	1	1	1	9	High Risk
Organization 2	2	2	2	2	2	2	2	2	2	18	Average
Organization 3	3	3	3	3	3	3	3	3	3	27	Low
Organization 4	1	1	2	1	2	2	2	2	2	14	High Risk
Organization 5	1	1	2	1	2	2	2	1	2	14	High Risk
Avg Score	1.6	1.6	2.0	1.6	2.0	2.0	2.0	1.6	2.0		
Risk Level	High Risk	High Risk	High Risk	High Risk	High Risk	High Risk	High Risk	High Risk	High Risk		

Max Risk 9
Lowest Risk 27
Avg Risk 18

Figure 2.11   Risk assessment tool.

become the norm. In retrospect, there are several takeaways from the previous examples. One, partnerships are a risky business. Two, not all partnerships are a good fit. Thus, organizations and their leaders must think ahead, measure, analyze and mitigate risks. Not knowing is no longer an option.

Three, risk definitely plays a role in the success or failure of organizational mergers, acquisitions and the like. As noted in the first example, culture differences disrupted the partnership efforts and cost both sides millions of dollars. Thus, risk is a relationship disruptor, not just normal current.

Finally, it is possible for leaders to risk assess potential partnerships and predict the success potential of coming together. With change, risk will always exist. However, leaders owe it to the organization and its stakeholders to ensure the rewards of partnerships far outweigh the risks. The only way this will happen is if simple risk tools are leveraged, valued and magnified by organizational leaders.

Simply put, leaders don't always know what they think they know. Perception is not always reality. Corporate partnerships are risky business. Thus, leaders must place risk at the top of the most wanted list to ensure they know when to run for the hills versus welcome partners into the family.

Reference

1. Harvard Business Review, 2011. *The New M&A Playbook*, Clayton M. Christensen, Richard Alton, Curtis Rising, Andrew Waldeck.

Chapter 3

Time: The Cardinal Sin of Failing to Use Time Wisely

Case Study: The Value of Studying Time—Is All Activity Value Added or Wasted Motion?

The Importance of Time

Is time study a worthy endeavor? Is the investment of studying how one uses their time worth the resource commitment? Does time really matter? Can time misused cost organizations large sums of money in waste and other opportunity costs? Is wasted time a hard dollar or only soft dollar savings opportunity? Does waste apply to time or is it just related to tangible items such as supplies, equipment and the like? Is time one dimensional or are there various ways to assess and use time? Do leaders really know what they think they know or is perception a false reality? Is the correct response always to add more people, thus dedicating more time to operational activities? We will answer these and more considerations in the following.

Time is the most valuable asset we have. Once it's gone, we don't get it back. Time can be viewed in increments such as spectrums, seasons or windows. Regardless of the view, time is a scarce resource that all leaders must use wisely.

Organizational thought leaders can assess time in many ways. The key here is, 'are you assessing how the organization's talent uses its time?' Figure 3.1 shows four organizational levels of the time spectrum that must be considered when studying time. Organizational levels can range from

DOI: 10.4324/9781003267966-3

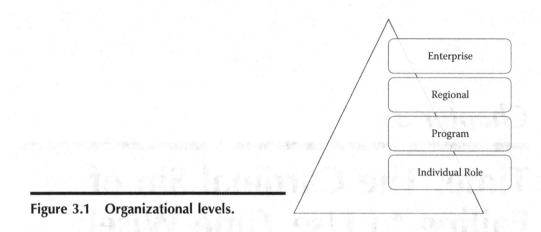

Figure 3.1 Organizational levels.

individual roles to the enterprise as a whole. The key here is to ensure all aspects of time are included in the study.

For years, myself and other thought leaders have heard organizational executives comment on how expensive meetings appeared to be for example. Another common response leaders often use is, 'we are overwhelmed and need more people to solve problems.' The key word here is people or formally referred to as full-time equivalents (FTEs). The real questions leaders should be asking themselves are following:

- Are all people in the organization spending their time wisely?
- What is the organization spending its time on organization wide, programmatically, regionally and even on the individual role level?
- Is our time being maximized or wasted?
- What percent of the organizational work hours are wasted?

These are just a few starter considerations when studying time. But, the takeaway is that leaders should challenge the status quo, measure, analyze and determine if the organization's time is adding value or just being wasted. It's been our experience that many times organizations and their leaders spend little to no effort studying how much time commitments actually cost their institutions. Thus, waste is ramped and quickly erodes the financial bottom line.

Waste is one of the most common sources of organizational inefficiency overlooked by enterprise leaders. The adage 'You don't know what you don't measure' applies here. Thinking back to Lean Green Belt training (IISE), there are eight wastes to be considered. Waste is essentially anything a customer is not willing to pay for.[1]

If an activity of any sort does not add value to the customer, then it's considered to be non-value add.[1] For this review, we will focus mainly on two aspects of waste: wasted motion and non-utilized talent. Wasted motion occurs when one moves more than is required. Thus, the activity does not add value to the customer. Non-utilized talent occurs when workers do not use their skills to their fullest capability.[1]

The key takeaway is that waste is bad and unhealthy for the organization. Leaders must identify, assess, analyze and eliminate waste at every turn. If not, waste will impede operations, directly impact the customer negatively at some point and cost the organization greatly in the long run. High performance is predicated on eliminating waste and working more efficiently.

Let's take a closer look at a few examples of time study to see if organizations were wasting their resources or getting the biggest bang for their buck.

Case Studies

Case Study 1

The first case study relates to an emergency ambulance service. This correlates to regional as noted in Figure 3.2. The scope of the service is many tens of thousands of customers annually over several geographic jurisdictions. This service is responsible for responding to thousands of emergency calls annually comprising gun shots, wrecks, strokes, heart attacks and the like. To say the least, this is a very high-risk business where every second counts. Thus, time is of the essence and very important.

The service historically used a regional deployment model to service its customers. The deployment model essentially placed ambulances in certain high priority call areas at certain times each day with the hope of having shorter response times to emergency calls. The deployment model sounded great in theory. But, it resulted in hundreds of workers annually spending excessive time driving from one location to another in hopes of the next call.

As an ambulance ran a call in a busy area of town, for example, another unit would be sent from a less busy area to the high call volume area to wait for the next call. In many instances, the next call would come in from a non-busy area. Thus, crews were driving back and forth all day and moving constantly. It is worth asking, is the activity really worth the gain? Arguably, not always.

Miles Driven Per Year	1,000,000
Fleet Cost Per Mile	$0.85
Total Fleet Costs	$850,000.00
Wasted Motion (miles)	150,000
% Miles Driven Wasted	15%
Annual $ Savings of Eliminating Wasted Motion (Fleet Costs)	$127,500.00
Time Traveling (60 mph base)	16,667
Time Traveling Wasted (60 mph base)	2,500
% Time Wasted Traveling	15%
Unit Hour Cost (4)	$200.00
Average $ Wasted Per Year Traveling	$500,000.00
Average $ Wasted Per Month Traveling	$41,666.67
Average $ Wasted Per Week Traveling	$9,615.38
Average $ Wasted Per Day Traveling	$1,369.86
Total Waste Savings (4)	$627,500.00

Figure 3.2 Fleet cost analysis.

The keys here are 'waiting' for the next call and 'moving' from one area to the next while not on an emergency call. Think back to the eight wastes of Lean. So, was this really an issue or did it add value to all customers? Let's see.

Figure 3.2 outlines a simple analysis of the ambulance service's time commitments in deploying and moving resources throughout its service area. The service drove over one million miles per year during normal daily operations. The fleet costs to the service were $0.85 per mile which totaled $850,000 per year. These fleet costs comprised fuel, tires, breaks, other routine maintenance for vehicles and the like.

The study revealed that 15% of the miles driven each year were wasteful. This equates to 150,000 miles of wasted motion. The dollar impact of this wasted motion was nearly $130,000 each year in fleet costs alone. Is this excessive? The short answer is yes.

The study also looked at waste from a time perspective in terms of utilized talent. If paramedics were sitting waiting for the next call or traveling from one point to the next in hopes of the next call, this relates back to both wasted motion and non-utilized talent. Simply put, they had skills that were not being used to the fullest extent.

The wasted miles per year resulted in at least over 2,500 hours of time wasted where staff were not using their skills sets. Instead, they were moving from one point to the next which did not add value much of the time. It costs the service roughly $200 per hour to run each ambulance. Thus, the average waste in time from a dollar perspective was $500,000. From a global perspective both wasted motion and non-utilized talent cost the organization nearly $630,000 per year in waste.

The lesson learned from this case study is that time matters. Waste and non-utilized time are very expensive to organizations and their customers. Moreover, leaders simply don't know that they don't measure. For years, the ambulance service leaders followed a theory related to deploying resources versus the data. In short, not all activity adds value and waste is an impediment to higher performance.

Case Study 2

This case study focuses on the program level as noted in Figure 3.3. A large service organization conducted a time study of a very significant and required program. Without this program, the enterprise could not provide services or function as a business. Also, the outcomes of the program directly impacted many tens of thousands of customers annually. The assessment began with the team that ran and facilitated the program. See Figure 3.3 for details.

Team Annual Salaries	$600,000.00
Total Team Work Hours Per Year	8,320
% of Team Time in Wasted Motion Per Year	70%
Team Salaries Wasted Per Year	$420,000.00
Team Salaries Wasted Per Month	$35,000.00
Team Salaries Wasted Per Week	$8,076.92
Team Salaries Wasted Per Day	$1,615.38
Team Hours Wasted Per Year	5,824
Team Hours Wasted Per Month	485
Team Hours Wasted Per Week	112
Team Hours Wasted Per Day	22

Figure 3.3 Time study.

The team's base salaries were roughly $600,000 per year. It was discovered with a time study of each team member, that 70% of the team's time was spent on wasteful activities. This relates back to wasted motion and non-utilized talent. The key here is that customers did not find value in or would not be willing to pay for these activities.

These wasteful activities cost the organization nearly $35,000 per month which equates to over $1,600 per day. Moreover, the waste in hours of work was nearly 6,000 per year. So, you may be wondering what is the point? Post analysis, the organization restructured the team, their roles and time commitments.

All the waste noted in Figure 3.3 was eliminated. The team quickly became a national best practice program site and did exponentially more with the same resources as before the restructure. The adage 'We need more people to solve our problems' was a perception, not reality. The organization achieved great gains by studying time, refocusing time commitments and spending the majority of its time adding value instead of just doing 'things.' In short, the small things matter and add up quickly.

Case Study 3

This case study relates to the individual role level as noted in Figure 3.1. A large organization was experiencing service and financial issues. Thus, an organizational study ensued to determine how the enterprise could accomplish more with less. Change agents were charged with this endeavor and began by reviewing a few critical roles to see what they spent their time on, how much of it actually added value and if opportunities existed.

See Figure 3.4 for details. The team found a diamond in the rough at the start. The first pilot batch of roles revealed that one had significant opportunity. The role worked 2,080 hours per year on average. The team found with a simple time study that 80% of the position's time was non-productive. This directly correlates to waste related to non-utilized talent. Simply put, skills existed that were not being used. Thus, value was being lost.

The annual salary for this position was $70,000. The stark reality was that $56,000 per year was being wasted for just one role. If the organization had thousands of workers, imagine what the enterprise cost in waste would be for time not used wisely. This waste converted to over 1,600 hours of non-productive hours per year.

Position Work Hours Per Year	2,080
% of Position's Time Non Productive	80%
Non Productive Time (Hours) Per Year	1,664
Annual Salary	$70,000
Annual Salary Wasted ($)	$56,000
Non Productive Time (Hours) Over 3 Years	4,992
Non Productive Time (Hours) Over 5 Years	8,320
Non Productive Time Costs Over 3 Years	$168,000
Non Productive Time Costs Over 5 Years	$280,000
Non Productive Time Costs Over 10 Years	$560,000

Figure 3.4 Role assessment.

Forecasting out a few years, this talent loss would cost the organization nearly $170,000 in three years and over $500,000 in a ten-year period. The key here is that leaders don't know what they don't measure. How long was this waste in practice? Unfortunately, for years.

A simple time study and analysis found hundreds of thousands of dollars of waste over a short time period for one role. Extrapolate this over a multi-thousand employee organization. How much money had and was the organization losing in lost time? Guaranteed, more than the leaders realized.

Case Study 4

The final case study relates to the enterprise level as noted in Figure 3.1. A large service organization experienced tremendous issues with managing its documents. This is a crucial aspect of performance improvement, but very non-glamorous to say the least. Many times, activities such as these never hit the top leadership radar and seem of little to no consequence to the organization.

This documented organizational knowledge was a requirement of creating a culture of standard work. Think of policies, procedures and the like. The end goal is ensuring a written process exists, is current and is accessible to all stakeholders when needed. Then, work is done the same way and correctly each time regardless of who performs the task.

The enterprise conducted a study, then transformed its document management system and process. Think of blow up the old and create the new world quickly. The new structure shifted away from manual processes to a system that automated and captured most of the work. This step allowed the organization to achieve great improvements in time, waste and customer outcomes.

The study focused on the enterprise as a whole. The organization was large and had many dozens of staff and leaders who handled documents daily in various work areas. These activities included creating, revising, reviewing, approving and reading policies, etc.

Figure 3.5 outlines some important details of the structure, process and outcomes. As noted, the enterprise had 30,000 document transactions per year. Pre-automation, each transition required 21 steps averaging at minimum at least five minutes per step. Post transformation, the new system required five steps averaging two minutes per step. The enterprise saved 16 process steps per transaction just by reworking process and leveraging technology.

These improvements saved 480,000 wasted motion steps each year. So, you may be wondering what's the big deal? Is this really a big deal or just another improvement? The study then focused on dollar impacts of this wastes.

In terms of time, the automation and new process saved 24,000 hours per year in labor. This equates to people manually updating, revising, approving

Number of Document Transactions Per Year	30,000
Number of Non Value Steps Per Transaction Pre Automation	21
Number of Steps Per Transaction Post Automation	5
Number of Wasted Motion Steps Saved Per Transaction Post Automation	16
Number of Steps Pre Automation Per Year	630,000
Number of Steps Post Automation Per Year	150,000
Number of Wasted Motion Steps Saved Post Automation Per Year	480,000
Average Time Saved In Transaction Post Automation (Min)	1,440,000
Average Time Saved In Transaction Post Automation (Hours)	24,000
Total Wastes Salary ($) Saved Post Automation	$600,000.00

Figure 3.5   Document transactions.

thousands of documents. The adage of paper pusher definitely applies here. The key lesson learned was that minor changes saved the organization $600,000 in salary costs per year.

The team learned again that leaders don't know what is not measured. Waste is a gnarly aspect of business that must be realized, assessed and dealt with quickly. Otherwise, it can sink the titanic (operationally speaking). The key is that time matters, is very costly in many ways and is worth the study.

Summary

After reviewing the case studies, it's obvious that studying time is a worthy endeavor. The investment of studying how one uses their time is worth the resource commitment. The stark reality is that we don't know what is not measured. Ignorance is not bliss in today's world. Change is the new norm and the market is demanding efficiencies now more than ever.

The only question is how many leaders will take the time to understand how valuable time is to their organization. The moral of the story is time really matters. It's finite and scarce. Moreover, time is very valuable and costly if not utilized properly. Leaders must realize that time has both hard dollar and soft dollar impacts on the organization and its stakeholders.

The case studies reveal that time is also multidimensional. Studying time needs several lenses. For thought leaders, a good starting point is assessing waste and time commitments for roles, programs, regions and the enterprise as a whole. Who would have ever thought process engineering concepts such as waste applied so heavily to time?

In summary, perception is not always reality. Thus, leaders must take time to learn what they don't know. Sometimes the elephant in the room is sitting right under our nose. The keys to mastering time are assessment, measurement, analysis and a bird's eye view of waste.

Reference

1. IISE, Lean Green Belt. 2016.

Catch or Release? Time Management Concepts Top Leaders Need to Succeed

Why Time Matters

Is time the most valuable resource we have? Can we get a day back once it's gone? Is it healthy for leaders to spend all their time problem solving or firefighting? Are all problems the same? Should leaders spend the same amount of time on all issues or are some more important than others? Can top leaders solve all the problems by themselves or is a team approach needed? Is delegation an art or science? Is delegation a friend or foe? Should organizational issues be risk prioritized before leaders own them (i.e., catch) or delegate (i.e., release) them? We will answer these and other questions in the following.

The reality is that time is an extremely rare commodity. Time can be defined as, 'the measured or measurable period during which an action, process, or condition exists or continues.'[1] The concept of time is synonymous with duration. The takeaway is that time is finite and limited in supply. Simply put, no one has a forever clock and leaders must ensure their time is used wisely. Thus, leaders must assess, plan and execute wisely to ensure they make the most of their time.

Time Management Concepts

The Leader Time Study

Have you ever stopped to think how much time you are spending working, solving problems, positioning the organization for success or looking forward versus in retrospect? It's surprising how much time leaders unknowingly invest in these activities. Let's take a closer look at a tool to assist leaders in considering their time commitments. See Figure 3.6 for details.

In Figure 3.6, there are four scenarios representing an average work schedule for leaders. This is simply a starting point considering schedules, time commitments and priorities will vary. Generally speaking, this concept will be applicable for many leaders. However, it can be modified for those anomalies.

The purpose is to outline the amount of time leaders actually spend on various activities. As we know there are only 365 days in a given year. It's a reasonable expectation for leaders to use a one-third measurement tool when

	Scenario 1	Scenario 2	Scenario 3	Scenario 4
Work Hours Per Day	8	10	12	14
Work Hours Per Week	40	50	60	70
Work Hours Per Year	2,080	2,600	3,120	3,640
Vacation Hours	80	80	80	80
Total Work Hours Per Year - Vacation	2,000	2,520	3,040	3,560
30 Year Career (Hours Worked)	60,000	75,600	91,200	106,800
Vacation: Average 2 Weeks (80 Hours)				
Days In a Year	365	365	365	365
Total Hours in a Day	24	24	24	24
Total Hours in a Week	168	168	168	168
Total Hours in a Year	8,736	8,736	8,736	8,736
Total Hours in a 30 Year Career	262,080	262,080	262,080	262,080
% of Time Working in a Day	33%	42%	50%	58%
% of Time Working in a Week	24%	30%	36%	42%
% of Time Working in a Year	23%	29%	35%	41%
% of Time Working in a 30 Year Career	23%	40%	49%	57%
Hours Problem Solving Per Day (Ideal < 20%)	1.6	2	2.4	2.8
Hours Problem Solving Per Week (Ideal < 20%)	8	10	12	14
Hours Problem Solving Per Year (Ideal < 20%)	400	504	608	712
Hours Problem Solving in a 30 Year Career (Ideal < 20%)	12,000	15,120	18,240	21,360
Hours Positioning the Organization Per Day (Ideal > 80%)	6.4	8	9.6	11.2
Hours Positioning the Organization Per Week (Ideal > 80%)	32	40	48	56
Hours Positioning the Organization Per Year (Ideal > 80%)	1,600	2,016	2,432	2,848
Hours Positioning the Organization in a 30 Year Career (Ideal > 80%)	48,000	60,480	72,960	85,440

Figure 3.6 Work hours.

assessing the time spent on life's activities. For example, and generally speaking, we tend to spend one-third of life sleeping, one-third of life working and one-third on life's other activities.

In Figure 3.6, if a leader works a typical 8-hour day it equates to the standard 40-hour work week. In this scenario, the leader would work roughly 2,000 hours per year if they take an average two-week vacation. Based on this schedule, the leader would spend 33% of their time working in a day. For an average day, 1.6 hours would be spent solving problems ideally. Moreover, 6.4 hours of their time each day would be spent on positioning the organization for future success. In the span of an average 30-year career, this leader would spend 12,000 hours problem solving and 48,000 hours positioning the organization for current and future success.

In the big picture, leaders are problems solvers. But, most importantly they are paid to lead the organization and its stakeholders forward. Thus, ideally should spend at least 80% of their time planning for the future, managing relationships and communicating with stakeholders to ensure the organization's vision becomes a reality.

The elephant in the room (so to speak) relates to the work hours per day. How many leaders actually spend just eight hours per day working? As noted in Figure 3.6, there are several scenarios. For leaders who spend ten or more hours working per day, they will spend many more hours per day, year and over the course of their careers solving problems or positioning the organization. Also, if leaders spend more than 30% of their time working other areas of life will suffer. Thus, their overall success will be impacted or hampered with time.

Subsequently, it's imperative for leaders to regularly assess their time, priorities and focal points. Time flies and often we don't know what we don't know until it's too late. If leaders spend the majority of their time firefighting or problem-solving, their probability of success in long term is minimal in the best-case scenario.

The Three Lens Approach

In order for leaders to master the art of time management and leverage it for ultimate success, they must view time through three lenses. Again, the intent is to ensure time spent is a value add for all stake holders. The first lens relates to what the leader can control. If a list of priorities is present or arises, the leader must list those items that can be controlled by the leader or team. The key is that those items the team can control should be the primary focus. It's reasonable for leaders to spend at least 80% of their time focused on these items.

The second lens relates to those priorities that the leader or team can influence. If the item(s) can be influenced by the team, then it's a reasonable expectation to spend less than 20% of the time on these focal points. The key to success here is for leaders to manage relationships, leverage data or other objective evidence to influence others. The end goal is to influence favorable outcomes and decisions involving other stakeholders for the team.

The third lens refers to those priorities that are only a concern. In short, the leader or team cannot control or influence these activities. Thus, the best course of action is place these items in the parking lot with frequent reviews.

Otherwise, the leader or team is wasting time focusing on and investing resources needlessly on priorities that they cannot affect.

Let's take a look at a simple example from the healthcare industry. Think of a team that works in operations. The team can control their work ethic, timeliness, accuracy, learning, contributions to the team's success, attitude, behavior and the like. Thus, 80% of their time should be focused on making these priorities the best they can be.

From a different view, the same team may only be able to influence items such as the division's or enterprise's goal-setting process. Therefore, the team would be wise to spend less than 20% of its time on these activities. In contrast, the team cannot control the federal government's decisions on industry policy related to reimbursement for certain health services. This would be something for the parking lot and needs little attention from the team.

Risk Prioritizer

Another very effective tool for leaders to leverage in time management is a risk prioritizer. Figure 3.7 outlines a very basic schematic that can be modified for specific organizational needs. The takeaway is that successful leaders will need to list their issues or priorities and update the list frequently. The risk prioritizer consists of at minimum five attributes: the issues, location (i.e., department, division, entity) of issues, the owner of the issues, risk level and action plan.

Issue	Location	Owner	Risk Level (1, 2 or 3)	Action Plan
Turnover	Dept. A	Leader A	2	TBD
Patient Falls	Dept. B	Leader B	1	TBD
Employee Injuries	Dept. C	Leader C	1	TBD

Risk Priority:
1. Threat to Life, Safety or Health
2. Critical to Mission
3. Important-Not a Risk to Life,
  Safety, Health or Mission

Figure 3.7 Risk prioritizer.

The whole premise with the tool is to answer the following:

- What's the issue?
- Where is the issue?
- Who owns the issue?
- What risk(s) do the issue pose to the organization and its stakeholders?
- What is or will be done to address the issue (short term and long term)?

In Figure 3.7, there are three items listed. They include employee turn-over, patient falls and employee injuries as examples. The most important focal point is that the risks category has three levels. Level one is a threat to life, safety and health. Level two risk is critical to mission for the organization to function and fulfill its operational purpose. Level three risk means the issue is important, but not a risk to life, safety, health or mission.

The key here is that the respective leaders would catch and focus on the level one risks first. Delegating these items would not be first priority. Moreover, these items would need to remain on the top leader's radar screen and be a top priority until resolved. The lesser risk item (i.e., turnover) could easily be delegated to other direct report leaders for resolution. The goal is to focus resources on the highest risks first.

Time Management Paradigms

The final time management tool relates to paradigms or leadership styles. See Figure 3.8 for details. There are three leadership time management paradigms: catch, release or both. In short, leaders who try to catch all the problems and solve them themselves is the first paradigm. This is an ineffective model of micromanagement that will quickly result in the leader becoming overwhelmed, less effective and burned out. This paradigm also creates trust and synergy issues with teams.

The next paradigm is categorized by leaders who mostly release or delegate. This is a very dangerous paradigm where leaders simply toss organizational issues to their direct report leaders blindly. This style of time management leadership can easily overwhelm direct reports, assign the wrong tasks to the wrong leaders who are under prepared and subsequently result in organizational failure. It's not uncommon for leaders here to meet less than 50% of their goals, have over 50% of their

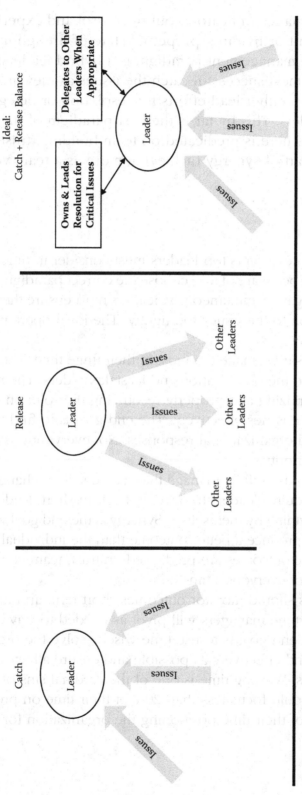

Figure 3.8 Leadership paradigms.

KPIs (key performance indicators) out of control and experience cyclical crisis management or live in a perpetual state of firefighting.

The ideal time management paradigm is a hybrid leadership style. Leaders who are most successful catch the issues as they arise, risk assess each one and then either lead efforts for resolution or delegate them to direct report leaders. This by far is the best paradigm of the three. However, success here is predicated on team building, trust, communication and the art of synergy (achieving more as a team versus individually).

Key Points

There are several key points top leaders must consider in time management. First, leaders must be aware of and choose the correct paradigm. The key here is not to over delegate. Simultaneously, leaders must ensure they do not micro manage or hold on to the issues too tightly. The ideal operating state is a balance of the two.

Second, leaders must make the most of their finite time. The key here is to know the risk(s) to the organization and its stakeholders. The middle ground of assessing, prioritizing and properly resourcing the solution response is imperative to solve issues effectively. The end goal is to find the right fit between risks and organizational responses. Not everything is an emergency or highest-level priority.

Third, leaders must artfully manage the people side of change to maximize their time. This requires leaders to develop trust. In short, leaders need teams and can't do everything by themselves. Synergy is the end goal where the parts working together produce a better outcome than the individual parts working in silos. Synergistic outcomes are predicated on trust, team cohesiveness and making the most of everyone's time.

Finally, leaders should monitor outcomes short term and long term. If needed, effective time managers will pivot as needed to stay on course and sustain wins. The end goal is to use time wisely, solve the organization's issues as timely and effectively as possible and ensure all activity adds value to all stakeholders. Wasting time is one of the cardinal sins of leadership. Ideally leaders should focus less than 20% of their time on problem-solving and at least 80% of their time positioning the organization for current and future success.

Summary

In today's world, change is the new norm and only constant. Thus, leaders must evolve with the times. Since time is finite and a limited resource, top leaders must use their time wisely to ensure success. The million-dollar question is how?

The keys to leadership success are focusing on what's really important, investing time on the most pertinent risks, leveraging trust with teams to accomplish more together and measuring to ensure wins and progress are sustained long-term. As we learned, time is the most valuable resource leaders have. No one has a forever clock and we cannot get a day back once it's gone. Thus, leaders must assess, prioritize and execute flawlessly to make the most of their time.

If leaders spend all their time problem solving or firefighting, they and their organizations will ultimately fail. Ideally, top leaders should spend at least 80% of their time positioning the organization for success via planning for the future, developing new ways of doing business, establishing and managing relationships along with a heavy dose of communication to stakeholders. Moreover, leaders should spend less than 20% of their time problem-solving. The key here is to spend more time looking ahead through the windshield versus focusing on the rear-view mirror.

In summary, leaders cannot do it all by themselves. All problems are not the same and top leaders cannot spend the same amount of time on all issues. To ensure success, leaders must position themselves for success. The reality is that successful time management is both an art and science. The art relates to the people side of leveraging talent to solve issues by focusing on what is important. The science relates to situational awareness of knowing what leaders are actually spending their time doing, if those activities are truly adding value and if the means will lead to a successful end.

Delegation is both a friend and foe. It's a friend if top leaders find the happy medium. Over-delegation can easily overwhelm direct reports, ensure top priorities are not a priority, grow organizational risks and stunt the organization's growth, forward progress or evolution. The best comparison is a mole hill that turns into a mountain or a bonfire that quickly grows into a forest fire.

Under-delegation is also an issue. Leaders who catch and own all the organization's issues will quickly become overwhelmed and ineffective. They essentially evolve into firefighters functioning in an emergency mode versus leaders thoughtfully guiding the organization with purpose. Again, the key is a balance between holding on to what is important and delegating what is appropriate.

The ultimate key for top leaders to succeed is to know when to catch and when to release. But, never lose sight of the organizations' issues, priorities and risks. Ignorance is not bliss. It's simply a one-way ticket on the disruption train.

Reference

1. Merriam-Webster, 2021. https://www.merriam-webster.com/dictionary/time

Chapter 4

Value: The Cardinal Sin of Not Understanding Value

Determining Leadership Net Worth: Do You Know Your Value to the Organization and Beyond?

Net Worth Defined

Net worth can be defined as, 'the value of all the non-financial and financial assets owned by an individual or institution minus the value of all its outstanding liabilities.'[1] In layman's terms, net worth is simply the net value leaders bring to the organization and its stakeholders. The key here is not to miss the term 'stakeholders.' We will cover this more later.

In many thought leadership circles, particularly healthcare, the basis of value is service, cost and quality. Simply put, the test has been, 'How does what we do as leaders improve service, cost and quality for each customer everywhere they touch the organization?' Is the work and outputs of any given leader adding value to internal and external stakeholders? If the answer is yes, then the next question relates to maximizing that value. How can we grow, maximize and replicate this value add across the enterprise? If the answer is no, then enterprise leaders must conscientiously consider a pivot of some sort.

DOI: 10.4324/9781003267966-4

The Process & Journey to Determining Net Worth

Recently, a top leader in healthcare was approached by a senior-level executive and asked to measure the impact of their program. The request was short, concise and very vague. Moreover, the request was not expected and quite strange to say the least. After some thought, the leader began to struggle with the concept of measuring their program's impact. Initially, thoughts centered around the concept of impact. What does impact really mean? Impact can be defined as, 'a significant or major effect.'[2]

The leader engaged a fellow thought leader for support and a very brief, but impactful study emerged. The leader in question was responsible for a very large and critical to mission program. This program was required for the healthcare enterprise to operate, generate income and simply provide services to many tens of thousands of customers. Without the program, the organization would not exist.

The challenge was that the leader historically took a traditional view of measuring impact. Traditionally, value was a measure of simply meeting or not meeting annual program goals. Unfortunately, this view is short cited and outdated. Thus, the leaders sought a much different course for a clearer and more comprehensive picture.

The Study's Structure

The first step of the study was to create a program portfolio which served as the canvas to paint the value picture. The portfolio consisted of four parts: program structure, program functions, outcomes to date and external knowledge sharing. See Figure 4.1 for details.

The program structure comprised a simple organizational chart coupled with a functional chart. These basics outlined who was on the team, who reported to whom and what functions or activities the team focused on.

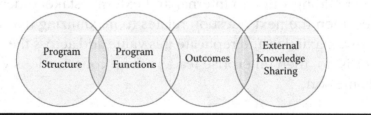

Figure 4.1   Portfolio basics.

The outcomes were tied to the programs main KPIs (key performance indicators). The KPIs were measured as frequently as possible with many being reviewed monthly at most. But, some unfortunately were reviewed on an annual basis based on the data available and nature of the program's business. It's important to note that each KPI directly or indirectly impacted stakeholder value.

Outcomes initially focused on the program's main KPIs, but later evolved. Historically, the program only measured its outcomes by either meeting or not meeting goal. There was no measurement of significance related to trends, improvements and the like. To further magnify outcomes, the team gathered its outcomes tied to externally sharing knowledge and its 'wins' outside the enterprise. These came in the form of presentations, publications and other knowledge sharing with industry peers across the globe.

The Study's Process & Outcomes

Once the program's structure was mapped out, the leaders began the journey to assess, measure and validate each aspect of the structure for its impact. Step one was to find benchmark data comparing the current program structure to its competitors in the geographic region. Surprisingly, the leaders discovered the program was much leaner than its competitors. Simply put, the leader's program produced comparable outputs with fewer resources. On further analysis, the leader's program was nearly half-million dollars more efficient in salaries alone compared to its largest competitor. Moreover, the program's outcomes were as good if not better in most arenas.

Step two was to define stakeholders. Simply put, who were they? What do they need, want and expect from the program? How satisfied are they from the program's services?

Defining stakeholders can be a tricky process. Many times, if leaders are asked who their customers are the knee-jerk reaction is the direct customer. In healthcare, for example, the immediate answer is the patients. Unfortunately, this is a short-cited view.

Each organization, regardless of business focus or industry, has both internal and external customers or stakeholders. Stakeholders encompass anyone, 'who is involved in or affected by a course of action'[3] of the business. For the impact study, the leaders created an exhaustive list of stakeholders including, but not limited to patients, families, staff, leaders, board members, the governing body, physicians, partner organizations, governments (local, federal, state), regulatory bodies, suppliers, vendors and the like.

The key here was to identify as many stakeholders as possible. Then, measure their satisfaction with the program's outputs. Let's focus on internal customers. The leaders sent out a very brief internal survey to hundreds of stakeholders annually. The survey focused mainly on attributes such as timeliness and overall satisfaction with the program. This feedback was used for program course correction, strategic planning and the impact study.

The outcomes were surprisingly good. The internal stakeholders overtime rated the program progressively better. Comparing the first internal survey to the last, both timeliness and overall satisfaction rates for example increased. Timeliness ratings increased by 13% and overall satisfaction ratings increased by 9%. Each survey attribute exceeded the 80% minimum satisfied goal for the survey. The takeaway was that the program's customers were highly satisfied with its outcomes.

Step three was to measure the program's main KPI over time to goal via run chart. Then, measure the significance of the KPI's trend over time. The main program KPI increased by over 40% in just a few years for several business units. Moreover, these improvements were significant at the 95% confidence level or higher. The direct impact on this improvement was related to safety and effectiveness of care and services to many thousands of sick, hurt and dying customers. The key here is that the program was more efficient, effective and produced better outcomes over time that impacted many tens of thousands of customers.

Finally, the team measured its impact on knowledge sharing. The team was very successful in publishing 'wins' and leveraging industry venues to share knowledge. Each publication was worth several thousand dollars in advertising alone for the enterprise. Over a short period of time, the team amassed a positive net contribution of over $300,000 in publications across the globe in various industry best practice venues. At the surface, the impact was great public relations for the enterprise. Looking further, these knowledge-sharing opportunities were more importantly a vehicle to impact the industry body of knowledge and help others adopt best practices to positively impact humanity across the globe.

The Showcase

Once the simple analysis was complete, a very simple showcase was created to magnify the program's impact. The results were assembled in both a larger portfolio document and executive summary. See Figure 4.2 for a sample executive summary. The goal was to provide a clear, concise and impactful summary that would accompany the detailed portfolio. In seconds, enterprise leaders would be able to glean better understanding of the program's impact, reach and outcomes.

Summary & Lessons Learned

In summary, the leaders learned a few very valuable lessons from a very simple study. One, we don't know what we don't measure. The adage 'measure twice and cut once' implies more wisdom that we often realize. There are many ways leaders and their teams provide value, but lack of measurement and magnification will ensure this value goes unnoticed.

Two, value comes in many forms other than just traditional goal attainment tied to revenue and costs. Yes, these traditional attributes are a good starter. But, there are various other value streams that positively impact stakeholders in many ways. As we learned in the analysis, the leader's program positively

Focus Area	Impact
Program Structure	• > $500,000 (more efficient than largest competitor)
Internal Voice of the Customer Survey • Program Timeliness • Program Overall Satisfaction *Both KPIs exceeded the 80% minimum KPI goal* *N=hundreds of internal stakeholders*	• 13% Improvement • 9% Improvement
External Knowledge Sharing *Organizational advertisement impact from publications*	• > $300,000
Main Program KPI *KPI Improvement statistically significant at 95% confidence level or higher* *KPI improvement correlated to improvements in safety and effectiveness of care and services*	• 40% Improvement
Program Reach	• 4 Continents
Primary Program Geographic Service Area	• Dozens of counties • > 200,000 stakeholders (minimum)
Revenues	• N/A
Program Costs	• Below Budget

Figure 4.2 Executive summary.

impacted various stakeholders and the industry as a whole in various parts of the world. These impacts were significant and directly contributed to the provision of safer more effective health services for many. Is this also a value add? Most definitely.

Three, leaders must be their own best advocates. Leaders must master the art and science of advocating for themselves, their teams and subsequent 'wins.' If outcomes are not considered or measured, then the leaders and their teams will never be recognized for these contributions. Moreover, the perception of leaders from their superiors and colleagues may be misguided due to a lack of knowledge of their organizational and industry contributions. The key is to measure everything, magnify wins at every turn, share knowledge outside the enterprise and advocate to ensure credit earned is credit received.

Is it possible to determine leadership net worth to an organization and its stakeholders? The short answer is yes. But, leaders should invest time to 'flesh out' and analyze the details so they don't sell themselves short. In today's world, the only constant is change. Leaders will be required to find innovative ways to add value to all stakeholders. Ignorance is not bliss and leaders will either succeed or fail by their ability to measure, improve, magnify and advocate.

References

1. Wikipedia, 2021. https://en.wikipedia.org/wiki/Net_worth
2. Merriam-Webster, 2021. https://www.merriam-webster.com/dictionary/impact
3. Merriam-Webster, 2021. https://www.merriam-webster.com/dictionary/stakeholders

The Value of Effective Leadership in High-Risk Environments

The Value of Leadership

Is leadership easy? Are all leaders the same? Is there a difference between effective and ineffective leaders? Is it possible to risk assess leaders on various critical elements? Will the level of risk determine how successful leaders are in the long run? Is all risk in leadership bad or does risk lead to better outcomes? Does a leadership title equate to someone being an effective leader or are other attributes required? We will answer these and other considerations in the following.

Leadership is simply the ability to get others to do what you want without force. Leadership is synonymous with influence and managing relationships. Merriam-Webster defines leadership as, 'a position as a leader of a group, organization, etc.' For one to be considered a true leader, there are several attributes that must be present.

One, leaders must have followers. Leading oneself simply does not qualify someone as a leader. Two, leaders must have a sense of direction so others know where to go. Life is not stagnant. Industries, markets and the world constantly change. Thus, so must the leaders that contribute to this movement.

Three, leaders must measure forward progress and add value to someone other than themselves. The key here is value. Value is anything a customer is willing to pay for.[1] In a value-centric industry, the customer is king. Thus, leaders must know who their customers are and what they perceive as a value add. Otherwise, leadership efforts will only be wasted motion.

Leadership is extremely important in every business. Leaders fill critical roles that have tremendous responsibility. Leaders are important for many reasons. First, they are charged with leading the organization. Second, they set the organization's course, make crucial decisions and directly impact the organization's success with those decisions. Moreover, they lead and influence people and their decisions affect all stakeholders of the organization. Finally, leaders leave legacies whether they be good or bad. These legacies directly impact the organization's brand for years to come. Thus, leaders are very valuable if they are effective in leading.

Leadership Value Contributions

Effective leaders are those who simply get the job done. The 'job' depends on the organization, industry, level and scope of organizational services. The key is for leaders to achieve a desired end via discharging their duties, achieving measurable results and adding value at every turn.

Ineffective leaders on the other hand are different. Many times, they are leaders in title only. They also struggle to influence others in moving to the desired end. Moreover, ineffective leaders often don't truly understand their customers and what value means to the end user. Thus, their approach, outcomes and value impact are ineffective.

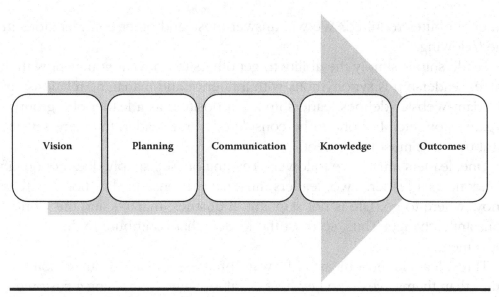

Figure 4.3 Leadership contributions.

Figure 4.3 outlines several contributions effective leaders provide to their organizations and their stakeholders. First, leaders set the organization's future direction with vision. Merriam-Webster defines vision as, 'the act or power of seeing.' The term is synonymous with lens. How one sees the future directly impacts their future direction. A vision simply outlines where the organization is and where it needs to go.

The key here is to ensure the customer is at the center of this foresight. Customer requirements do and should help shape the organization's future plan. Otherwise, the aim will always be off target. Consequently, leaders will be ineffective.

Second, leaders contribute to value by leading organizational planning. A vision must be accompanied by a plan in order to become a reality. Leaders who can create plans that identify risks, add value to all stakeholders, move the organization in the desired direction, produce operational outcomes that customers value and the like will be more effective than their counterparts. In contrast, planning that is leadership focused is not ideal and often is a non-value add for the customers.

Third, leaders contribute to organizational success via communication. Communication can be a very powerful vessel if leveraged properly. One key to consider is communication direction. Effective leaders who add value are those who can communicate vertically and horizontally.

This simply means they can communicate effectively with information that resonates to all stakeholders regardless of title, status, rank or position in the enterprise. This includes peers, subordinates and superiors. The adage 'always know your audience' applies here. It's a must that leadership communication be tailored to the audience at hand.

It is also important to consider communication effectiveness. Did stakeholders just listen or actually hear the message and its intent? Hearing connotates that someone listened and absorbed the message with an understanding of its purpose. The key here is for leaders to communicate with intent and a deep understanding of the audience's perspective. Otherwise, leadership communication is ineffective and simply noise.

Fourth, leaders provide knowledge. For the sake of this conversation, knowledge can be viewed in two dimensions: internal and external. The first step is for leaders to possess knowledge. This comes through years of learning, trials, tests and successes. Deep wisdom is a result of various life challenges that produce great understanding.

The next attribute is sharing knowledge. Leaders share knowledge internally to the organization's stakeholders via communications, decision making, teaching, projects and the like. Effective leaders also share knowledge externally. External knowledge transfer may come in the form of presentations at industry venues, publications or other best practice work. The key here is that leaders should effectively share the knowledge, impact the way the industry conducts business and add greater value to those outside the inner circle.

Finally, effective leaders add value to the outcomes they produce. Success must be measured. There are several outcomes that are commonly considered here. Most often leadership effectiveness is tied to core value streams such as service, cost and quality. Does the leader set respectable goals in these arenas and meet or exceed those goals? If so, then the leader is effective.

Other measures of success or effectiveness may be organizational specific. One example could be a leader's ability to influence donors to contribute to a building campaign for a new hospital. Can the leader legitimately influence other stakeholders to donate funds that will be used to care for sick, injured and dying customers via a new hospital? If so, then the leader is effective.

If not, then the leader may lose political capital, influence and be less effective. There are many examples too numerous to mention. The takeaway is that the 'proof is in the pudding.' Outcomes matter and are directly correlated with leadership effectiveness in adding value.

The Leadership Risk Assessment

If change is the new norm and produces risk as its byproduct, organizations must assess the level of risk each leader contributes to the operation. See Figure 4.4 for details. Figure 4.4 represents the leadership risk assessment tool with an effectiveness focus.

Step one is for the enterprise to list the leaders of interest in column one. Then, rank each leader on various attributes.

- *Goal Setting*-Determine if the leader is effective with setting goals. Are the goals relevant, measurable, achievable and the like? Can the leader set goals that resonate with the organization's stakeholders, etc.? If yes, then the score is 1. If no, the leader receives a 2.
- *Communication*-Is the leader an effective communicator? Is the leader's message heard or just noise? Does the leader effectively communicate with all stakeholders regardless of status, title, role or location? Each leader is ranked on this attribute as noted in Figure 4.4.
- *Vision*-Is the leader's vision ideal for the organization and its customers? Is the future plan aligned with market direction and realistic? Is the leader a visionary or just a hopeless romantic? Each leader is ranked accordingly.
- *Significant Outcomes*-Has the leader produced significant outcomes tied to the value equation. There are two notables here: significance and value. Significance is related to the statistical significance of the outcomes data. It's imperative to ensure improvement is truly that improvement. The adage 'two data points don't make a trend' applies here. The key is to ensure the outcomes are statistically sound, true improvements and sustained long-term. The ranking options are noted in Figure 4.4.
- *Knowledge Sharing*-Is the leader knowledgeable of industry expectations, best practices and the like? Is this knowledge shared internally and externally? If the answer is yes, then the score is 1. If no, then a 2 is applied.

Leader	Goal Setting (1=Yes; 2=No)	Communication (1=Yes; 2=No)	Vision (1=Yes; 2=No)	Significant Outcomes (1=Yes; 2=No)	Knowledge Sharing (1=Yes; 2=No)	Risk Score *Sum Columns 2-6 Lower Score = LowerRisk	Risk Level
Leader 1	2	1	2	2	2	9	High Risk
Leader 2	1	1	2	2	2	8	Average
Leader 3	2	2	2	2	2	10	High Risk
Leader 4	2	2	2	1	1	8	Average
Leader 5	1	1	1	2	2	7	Ideal
Leader 6	2	2	2	2	2	10	High Risk
Leader 7	1	1	1	1	1	5	Ideal
Leader 8	2	2	2	2	2	10	High Risk
Leader 9	1	2	1	2	1	7	Ideal

Ideal Risk Goal   5

Max Risk   10

Avg Risk   8

Figure 4.4   **Leadership effectiveness risk assessment tool.**

Once the enterprise assesses each attribute for each leader, the risk tool provides the risk score. The key here is that the lower the score, the lower the risk to the organization. Simply put, less risk is better. Each risk score has an associated risk level as noted in Figure 4.4. These risk levels include: high, average and ideal.

Let's view the leadership risk assessment tool practically. The organization chose nine leaders to assess their risk of being effective or not. Once the leader cohort was scored for each attribute, 33% of the leaders were ranked as ideal. This simply means they are low-risk leaders. Thus, they have the greatest probability in succeeding in the value attributes noted in the figure. If the leaders succeed, so shall the enterprise.

In contrast, 44% of the leaders were high risk of not successfully maneuvering goal setting, communication, vision, outcomes and sharing knowledge. This is a signal that these leaders have a greater probability of failure. It's important for the organization to consider several thoughts here:

- Are the leaders in the right role?
- Do they need coaching, training or mentoring?
- Are other resources needed for these high-risk leaders to become more effective?

The takeaway is that some form of action is required to mitigate the risks and avoid value loss. The solution will depend upon a more in-depth process. However, this risk will impact both the organization and its customers unfavorably if not addressed judiciously.

Summary

The lesson learned is that leadership can be very challenging, but rewarding if maneuvered properly. Organizations and their leaders simply don't know what they don't measure. Risk is a stark reality of today's market which does not seem to be leaving anytime soon. As noted, change is the new norm. The more prevalent change and its affects are, the greater level of risk organizations will face. Thus, organizations must risk assess the potential for their leaders to be effective. Otherwise, adding value will only be a pipe dream.

The reality is that leadership is learned and cultivated over time. Effective leaders must possess capabilities such as vision, planning, sharing knowledge and the ability to produce outcomes in high-risk environments. It can't be overstated that, 'the bigger the risk, the bigger the reward.'

Not all leaders are effective. Those front-runners who can master the art of assessing, mitigating and preventing risks from spilling over into the organization's value streams will be much more effective than those who cannot. In the long run, what matters most is ensuring the enterprise is positioned properly, meets and exceeds customer expectations and adds value at every turn. Otherwise, the activity is just operational noise that is ineffective.

In summary, leadership is more than a title or position. It's really the ability to convince others to do what you want without force. Thus, effective leaders will have to master many attributes or run the risk of being ineffective.

Reference

1. IISE, Lean Green Belt. 2016.

The Value of Goals: Are They Rudders or Anchors?

The Value of Goals

Are all goals equally important? Is there a right and wrong way to set goals? Is it possible to risk assess organizational goals? Do goals provide the same level of value regardless of focus, relevancy or structure? Is goal attainment a primary indicator of leadership success? Do all organizational goals resonate with its stakeholders? Are there several organizational levels to consider when creating high-value goals? Are some goals higher risk to the organization and its stakeholders than others? We will answer these and other considerations in the following.

Goals are, 'the end toward which effort is directed.'[1] In layman's terms, goals are the desired end that leaders intend to achieve. Goals can also be viewed as a mechanism to accomplish something. Moreover, goals can also be a rudder for the organization if handled correctly steering it to the desired end. In contrast, goals can also function as anchors preventing the organization from moving forward. The takeaway is that goals are important and have great impact on organizational success and customers.

The question to be answered is, what is the difference between goals and goals that add value? Value is simply anything a customer is willing to pay for.[2] If goals don't add value to the customer, then they can be categorized as non-value add. It's important to note that in any organization customers cannot be defined from a silo perspective.

In reality, a customer is anyone that touches the organization at any touchpoint. There are also direct and indirect customers. For example, a direct customer of a local restaurant is the person who arrives at the drive through for food. In comparison, an indirect customer for the same restaurant could be a citizen in the same county who receives some benefit from the local sales tax that the restaurant pays to the local government.

Irrespectively, customers can include direct customers, governments, regulatory agencies, communities, staff, leaders, family members of direct customers and the like. The key is for leaders to know who their customers are and what they want. Otherwise, value-added goals will always be an elusive target. Thus, leaders will struggle and more than likely fail long-term.

Goal Levels

There are several levels of goals worth noting. See Figure 4.5 for details.

First, organizational leaders typically create strategic goals initially. These are typically referred to as enterprise goals. This is a 30,000-foot view, organizationally speaking. The purpose of high-level strategic goals is to set the organization on the right course and provide leaders and staff a base to

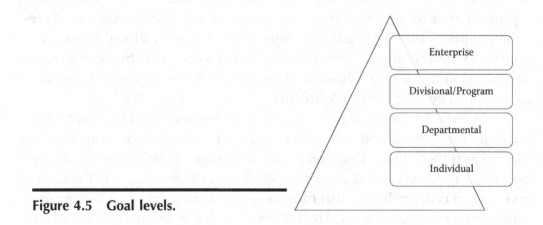

Figure 4.5   Goal levels.

determine their goals. The desired end is for the organization as a whole to meet customer expectations around attributes such as quality, service, cost and the like.

Second, organizational leaders on the divisional level focus on goals directly affecting their level. However, their goals must be aligned and relevant to enterprise goals. The key is relevant. The further down the organizational chart leaders reside, the greater relevance of goals must exist. Divisional leaders must be able to translate the intent of enterprise leaders goals to lower level leaders and staff. Otherwise, the organization's efforts will be off target.

Third, goals are considered at the departmental level. Departmental leaders are extremely important to creating goals that add value. The main reason is that front-line leaders and staff are closest to the process that impacts the customer. They simply know better than most what the customer values. Thus, their insight will ensure the creation of tangible goals that will guarantee the organization is successful in adding value to every customer.

Finally, leaders must help front-line staff set realistic goals that correlate to the overarching enterprise goals. Again, individual goal setting can never be overlooked. It's a fact that if front-line staff and leaders are off target, so will be the organization as a whole. Thus, individual goals are as important as any other level noted in Figure 4.5.

Goal Focus Areas

In addition to levels, goals have many focus areas. These focus areas tend to be tied directly to the organization's strategic plan. Sample goal focus areas include, but are not limited to attributes such as quality, service, finances (cost, revenue, profit margin, capital expenses), learning, improvement, people and the like. Let's take a look at a couple of examples.

Commonly, people goals can be linked to turnover for example. This is only one example of many. The goal is for organizational leaders to experience less turnover in their operations. Turnover, many times, can result in issues with service and cost. Thus, eroding value the organization provides, its culture and the level of goal attainment.

Another example relates to service. Regardless of industry, most organizations set service goals linked to customer satisfaction. Leaders don't know what they don't measure. Thus, it's imperative for leaders to know what their customers think of the organization and its subsequent services provided.

There is no better lens than that of the customer. The adage 'being a hero in our mind' applies here. Many times, the leadership perspective is short cited. Unfortunately, we may perceive all we do as a value add. However, customers may experience blind spots that are not a value add. It's important to obtain, analyze and quickly respond to customer feedback.

Risk Assessment Tool

The most important aspect of goal setting is the risk assessment. In today's world, change is the only constant. Thus, risk is a dominant player in operations. If leaders do not consider risk in the goal-setting process, goal attainment may be stifled and only a distant desire instead of an achieved end.

See Figure 4.6 for details. The risk assessment for goals is easier than it sounds. Simply put, there are two ways to use this tool. The first lens relates to leadership. If the enterprise leaders desire to assess the level of risk with a leadership subgroup, then the tool works great for this.

Step one is to list the leaders in the subgroup. Then, assess each leader on the following attributes noted in Figure 4.6. Each attribute is ranked based on a yes or no response. Considerations are as follows:

- Are the leader's goals aligned with the organization's mission?
- Are the leader's goals scalable? This simply means if the goals are applicable at all levels in the organization as noted in Figure 4.6.
- Are the goals directional? Directional goals help move the organization forward. Typically, high performing organizations will set base goals as minimum performance expectations. Then, stretch goals to be attained once the base goals are met.
- Are the goals relatable? Simply put, can everyone in the enterprise relate to the goals and practically apply them in their work areas? This applies to all levels from the governing board to individual front-line leaders and staff.
- Are the goals attainable or realistic? There is nothing worse than setting goals that are not realistically attainable. This simply erodes morale and sets people up for failure. Thus, forward progress is stifled.

Leader	Goals Aligned with Mission? (1=Yes; 2=No)	Goals Scalable? (1=Yes; 2=No)	Goals Directional? (1=Yes; 2=No)	Goals Relatable? (1=Yes; 2=No)	Goals Attainable? (1=Yes; 2=No)	Goals Comparable to Best Practices? (1=Yes; 2=No)	Risk Score *Sum Columns 2-7 Lower Score = Lower Risk	Risk Level
Leader 1	1	2	2	2	1	1	9	Average
Leader 2	2	2	2	2	2	2	12	High Risk
Leader 3	1	1	1	1	1	1	6	Ideal
Leader 4	1	2	1	2	1	1	8	Ideal

Ideal Risk Goal	6
Max Risk	12
Avg Risk	9

Figure 4.6 Goal risk assessment tool.

Once these attributes are rated, the tool provides a risk score. The key here is that the lower the risk score the lower the risk. Thus, the enterprise should strive to ensure all leaders are ideally setting goals that meet these attributes at each level of the organization. Otherwise, the organization is at risk of not meeting customer expectations tied to service, quality and cost. Therefore, value will be only a distant desire instead of the achieved end.

Let's look at the risk tool from a practical perspective. Of the four leaders, 50% scored yes on each attribute. This means the leaders are low risk of not meeting goals. Moreover, they have the greatest chance of contributing to the organization's success and long-term viability. This appropriate organizational response is to empower these leaders for success and invest few resources in managing these goals. The lower the risk, the more autonomy the leaders should be granted to move forward in operationalizing their goals.

In contrast, 25% of the leaders are average risk and the remaining 25% is high risk. The key here is that enterprise leaders should pivot and help the high-risk leaders with goal setting. Thus, ensuring the organization has the greatest chance of adding the greatest amount of value.

The other perspective of the risk tool focuses on goals themselves. See Figure 4.7 for details. From a practical example, leaders simply list each goal. Then, assess each goal for the listed attributes in columns 2–7. The tool then provides the risk score.

Again, the lower the score the less risk. Leaders should focus on the high-risk goals to ensure a pivot resets these goals on the right track. If not, it's likely that goals will not be achieved. Thus, they function as an anchor which prevents the organizational ship from sailing forward to the safe haven out of the storm.

Summary

The reality is that change is the new normal. As change becomes common place, so will risk become the norm and even increase under certain circumstances. The key is for leaders to understand their risk as it relates to goal setting. Leadership success is predicated on realistic, aligned, scalable and directional goals that will move the organization in the right direction.

High-risk goals and leaders who own them will quickly become organizational anchors if not identified, mitigated and adjusted. The key here is we

Goals	Goals Aligned with Mission? (1=Yes; 2=No)	Goals Scalable? (1=Yes; 2=No)	Goals Directional? (1=Yes; 2=No)	Goals Relatable? (1=Yes; 2=No)	Goals Attainable? (1=Yes; 2=No)	Goals Comparable to Best Practice? (1=Yes; 2=No)	Risk Score *Sum Columns 2-7 Lower Score = Lower Risk	Risk Level
Goal 1	1	2	2	2	1	1	9	Average
Goal 2	2	2	2	2	2	2	12	High Risk
Goal 3	1	1	1	1	1	1	6	Ideal
Goal 4	1	2	1	2	1	1	8	Ideal

Ideal Risk Goal 6
Max Risk 12
Avg Risk 9

Figure 4.7 Risk tool.

don't know what we don't measure. Thus, the adage 'measure twice and cut once' applies here. In contrast, low-risk goals and their respective leaders have the greatest probability of being successful. As noted, effective goals are rudders that help steer the organization forward. As a result, it's imperative that organizations ensure goal setting is a value driver instead of a deterrent to forward progress.

In summary, all goals are not equally important. High-risk goals should take priority over their counterparts. The right way to set goals is simply determine what the customer needs, wants and desires. Then, set goals that meet the aforementioned attributes. Finally, risk assess each goal and its respective leader to ensure the outcomes grow the organizational pie and add value at every turn. The key takeaway is that change and risk if not handled correctly can easily be the kryptonite that erodes organizational value. Thus, leaders must risk assess and respond judiciously to succeed.

References

1. Merriam-Webster, 2021. https://www.merriam-webster.com/dictionary/goal
2. IISE, Lean Green Belt. 2016.

The Value of Sustainability—Leveraging Improvement Methodology to Impact Humanity Long-Term

The Concept & Journey

In the improvement world, one of the hardest crafts to master is sustainability. The best comparison of a sustainable process or outcome relates to its ability to be maintained or supported long-term.[1] Sustainability is much easier said than done. Over the years, many process experts or change agents have struggled to sustain improved outcomes. The real question is why?

Recently, a change agent presented a series of outcomes for a large health system to a group of senior leaders. The topics of discussion centered around safety and effectiveness of services, quality outcomes and the like. Fortunately, there were a lot of positive wins to discuss from various areas of the enterprise. However, sustained results were not the norm.

The obvious trend was that leaders and change agents were very good at identifying issues, deploying resources and improving 'something.' But, many of the outcomes were not sustained long-term. A small team decided to sponsor a pilot project with the intent of identifying those areas and attributes that sustained improvement 'wins' long-term better than others. Furthermore, and most importantly, determining why only a limited number of entities were so successful in maintaining these outcomes longer term as compared to their counterparts.

The first phase of the pilot began with the team creating a journey map. The journey map process began with a simple theory. Those hospitals that learned, implemented and championed improvement methodologies strategically realized more sustainable outcomes overtime. They simply matured at a higher rate than their counterpart hospitals. The group chose two hospitals as the focus areas for the pilot study.

Both entities were very similar in scope, size and geographic service areas. But, they varied in the services they provided to the region. Each impacted tens of thousands of customers each year, respectively. They also served various communities in their respective regions of the state. Moreover, each had a Six Sigma Black Belt trained top leader.

As the team progressed with the study, several keys emerged. See Figure 4.8 for details.

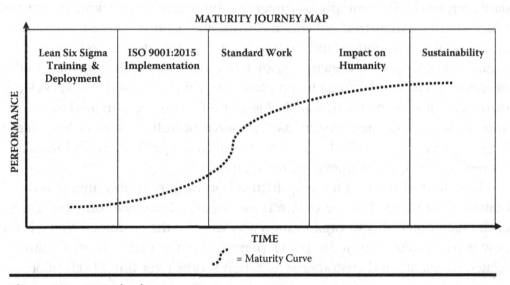

Figure 4.8   Maturity journey map.

First, the successful entities followed a five-step journey to sustainability. Step one involved training leaders and staff in improvement methodologies such as Lean, Six Sigma and the like. Once training occurred, the resources were deployed to improve 'something' tied to service, cost or quality. These two hospitals produced respectable lists of significant improvement outcomes in these arenas.

The results were measurable, tangible to customers and statistically significant. Moreover, they significantly outperformed their counterpart hospitals in volume of 'wins' and the sustainment of outcomes long-term. The pearl was culture. They were more inclined to learn and apply methodologies correctly as compared to their counterpart entities.

Second, the successful hospitals became ISO 9001:2015 certified and magnified this methodology with their Lean Six Sigma base. Simply put, they added more weapons to the improvement arsenal. ISO 9001:2015 was extremely helpful in focusing on a top leadership approach to improvement with a heavy emphasis on risk-based thinking and evidence-based decision making. These concepts sound like the norm, but are often overlooked by leaders. In short, the addition of ISO 9001:2015 forced top leaders to own the current state, identify internal and external risks constantly and use data to justify decisions or lack thereof.

The third phase of the journey related to standard work. The successful hospitals that were really good at sustaining outcomes did better with standardizing work. They simply documented the organization's knowledge and processes in standardized policies and work instructions. These tools allowed all stakeholders to understand how to do work consistently and correctly regardless of role, experience or knowledge base. Once the organization's processes were standardized in templates, they were housed in a knowledge management system. Then, stakeholders at all levels were trained to use the knowledge management system as the source of truth or well of knowledge for completing work. The focus here was accuracy, efficiency and standardization of work at each level of the hospital.

Phase four of the journey map focused on each hospitals impact on humanity. At the end of the day, service organizations have one test. Does each touch point of your organization add value to the customer? Value is the new gold standard. From the pilot's perspective, the main focus of value related to quality and customer satisfaction scores over time. Both pilot hospitals trended higher over time in these arenas as compared to their counterparts.

The last phase was sustainability. Were leaders able to sustain the wins, improvement in quality or customer satisfaction and standard work long-term? Simply put, did the end justify the means? To qualify as a top sustainer, the hospitals had to sustain improvements two years or longer. Both pilot hospitals were able to produce progressively better outcomes for several years running as compared to their counterparts.

The Data

As the pilot team progressed with the study, they analyzed various data to justify the assumptions tied to each phase of the journey map previously noted. First the team trended value scores for each hospital over a multi-year period. See Figure 4.9 for details.

The value scores represented customer satisfaction and quality scores such as infections, harm, falls, mortality and the like. Each entity listed up to a dozen KPIs in a showcase with current and historical performance to goal each month. The team took it one step further and created an aggregate score for each hospital. This maturity value score represented the percentage of quality and customer satisfaction scores attained each month.

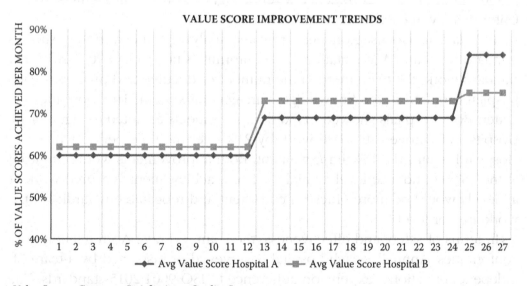

Value Score = Customer Satisfaction + Quality Scores
N > 100,000 Customer Encounters

Figure 4.9   Value score trends.

Attribute	Focus	Hospital A	Hospital B
Value Score Improvement	Impact on Humanity	10%^	9%*
Standard Work Improvement	Standardization, Accuracy & Efficiency	21%^	15%*
Accreditation Non-Conformity Reductions	Safety & Effectiveness of Services	-25%	-47%

* = *Significant at 95% Confidence Level*
^ = *Significant at 99% Confidence Level*

Value Score = Customer Satisfaction + Quality Scores
N > 100,000 Customer Encounters

Figure 4.10 Aggregate view.

Simply put, leaders viewed each hospital's monthly performance at a glance. The question to be answered was simple. What percentage of quality and service scores are we meeting? Is the trend improving over time or not? If the answer was yes, then the team accelerated. If no, then a pivot was required.

This aggregate view was a simple indicator as to if improvement efforts were working or not. As noted in Figure 4.10, both hospitals showed marked improvement over a multi-year period. Each year, they achieved more goals than the year before tied to quality and customer satisfaction. This pattern fortunately progressed and improved over time for these pilot hospitals. As noted in Figure 4.10, Hospital A's value scores improved by 10% while Hospital B's improved by 9% for the time period. These improvements were significant at the 95% confidence level or higher as noted in Figure 4.10. Unfortunately, their counterparts were not so lucky.

The team also focused on measuring and analyzing other attributes such as standard work and Accreditation non-conformities tied to ISO 9001:2015. For standard work, the team trended the number of documented processes each hospital captured in the knowledge management system. The more the better. Both hospitals showed marked improvements as noted in Figure 4.10. Hospital A improved standard work by 21% over the time period while Hospital B realized a 15% improvement. Both improvements were significant at the 95% confidence level or higher. These achievements ensured work at all levels would be more efficient, consistent and repeatable regardless of work area or level.

In terms of safety and effectiveness, the team leverage Accreditation non-conformities. Annually, each hospital is surveyed or inspected by a team of independent national experts on adherence to ISO 9001:2015 standards. The main focus of the surveys is to ensure each hospital is meeting federal safety and effectiveness requirements. The metric of focus was non-conformities. If the survey teams find any deficiencies to federal requirements, they issue non-conformities. The entity leaders must resolve each non-conformity in a very short time to continue to operate. Each hospital is required to be accredited in order to operate and receive reimbursement for services provided. In short, the end game is to receive fewer non-conformities each year. Thus, the hospital provides safer more effective care and services.[2]

A deeper dive revealed that both hospitals improved Accreditation non-conformities during the time period. Hospital A realized a 25% reduction in non-conformities while Hospital B realized a 47% reduction. The takeaway was that each hospital was providing safer more effective care and services to many thousands of customers annually. Thus, the impact on humanity was increasing for the better as time passed.

Summary & Lessons Learned

As we look back on the case study, there are several questions worth considering. Does sustaining improvement wins really matter? Does improvement methodology really work? Is it feasible to measure improvement impacts on humanity? Can customer value be measured, improved and sustained long-term?

The short answer to all questions posed is simply yes. All improvements should be sustained long-term. Otherwise, the activity, resource commitment and time engaged to improve is essentially non-value add. Second, yes improvement methodologies really do work. The big focal point here is 'if.' They work 'if' leaders support improvement, understand how to apply the methodology and champion initiatives. Without cultural alignment, it's hard to achieve wins and sustain them in long term. As we know, leadership sets culture and culture determines whether the enterprise will be successful long-term.

Third, yes thought leaders can most definitely measure impacts on humanity and the value they receive from improvement efforts. At the end of the day, businesses succeed or fail based on their ability or lack thereof to provide value to each customer everywhere they touch the business. Moreover, service industries such as healthcare most definitely impact humanity far greater than most realize. One bad process or lack of a good process can dissatisfy, harm or even worse. Thus, understanding one's customers and knowing what they want from a data-oriented position is vital to meeting and exceeding customer requirements through value.

Finally, the case study provided a few keys worth summarizing. The hospitals that were able to improve and sustain those wins had several attributes. One, the top leader was trained as a Six Sigma Black Belt. The pearl is that knowledge matters. More importantly is the ability to apply that knowledge. The higher performing hospitals learned and applied methodology better than their counterparts.

Also, methodology really works and directly impacts humanity if leverage properly. Both hospitals in the study realized significant improvements in safety and effectiveness, quality and customer satisfaction. Fortunately, these wins were sustained and improved upon over time. Thus, humanity benefited in many ways and the impacts in some facets were immeasurable.

In summary, there is value in sustaining outcome improvements. It's hard to improve what is not measured. The key for thought leaders, change agents and the like is to know your numbers, leverage data to see the forest for the trees and ensure value is being added at every turn. Otherwise, improvements will never be realized or only short-lived. Thus, the end will not justify the means.

References

1. Merriam-Webster, 2021. https://www.merriam-webster.com/thesaurus/sustainable
2. American Society for Quality (ASQ), *'How ISO 9001 Helped a Georgia Health System Provide Safer More Effective Care.'* 2020, Bedgood, Casey.

Chapter 5

Knowledge: The Cardinal Sin of Lacking Knowledge Fundamentals & Failing to Share Knowledge

Knowledge 2.0: Talent Tools Visionary Leaders Must Have to Succeed in High-Risk Environments

Knowledge 2.0

Change is the new normal and only constant. One side effect or consequence of change is risk. Risk can be defined as the 'possibility of loss or injury.'[1] The reality of risk is that there are two sides, generally speaking. Upside risk essentially means the risk is associated with some benefit. In contrast, downside risk is commonly associated with some level of loss. In high-risk environments, leaders must necessitate goals to maximize benefits and minimize loss.

But, how will leaders deal with risks properly? Ignorance is not bliss in today's world. Hosea (4:6 KJV) puts it this way: 'My people perish for a lack of knowledge.' One key for visionary leaders to thrive in uncertain markets laden with risk is knowledge. Knowledge can be defined as, 'the fact or condition of knowing something with familiarity gained through experience or association.'[2] In layman's terms, knowledge is what people know based on their life and business experiences. The reality is that deep knowledge or wisdom comes with time and through trials, tests and opposition.

There are several thoughts worth considering. Will basic knowledge allow leaders to succeed in high-risk environments? Are there critical factors of organizational knowledge that leaders must master to succeed? Do you know where your organizational knowledge gaps are and what level of risk they pose? What percentage of your organizational roles could retire tomorrow? How many are critical roles that the organization must have to survive and thrive? Does your organization have a global knowledge process to ensure organizational knowledge is accessible, relevant, actionable and leveraged to deal with market risks?

Let's take a closer look at a few tools that will help leaders ensure their organizational knowledge is top notch, industry leading and being shared appropriately.

Knowledge Tools

Critical Factors of Organizational Knowledge

One tool leaders need in their organizational jump bag is a brief outline of critical factors that impact organizational knowledge. See Figure 5.1 for details. The first critical factor of knowledge is talent. Everything in current

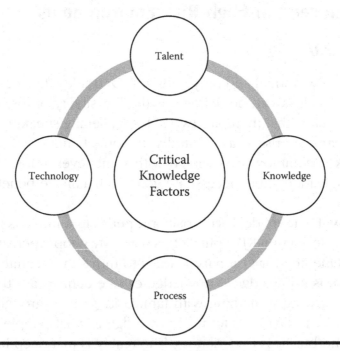

Figure 5.1 Organizational knowledge critical factors.

industry begins and ends with people. In recent years, many leaders have referred to their people as teammates, colleagues, human resources and the like.

In reality, talent is simply the vessel in which every organization stores its knowledge. People are the most valuable asset of any organization. The goal of leadership and their respective organization should be to maximize their talent. In order to do this, leaders must wisely hire, train, retain, reward and elevate their top talent. Otherwise, someone else will.

The second critical factor of organizational knowledge is knowledge. Knowledge is simply reflected in developed talent. Top performing organizations invest significant time, resources and plans on developing talent. This development may take the form of education, training, experience and knowledge sharing. The takeaway is that knowledge matters is valuable and portable. The more you know, the better.

The third critical factor is process. Does your organization have a process to capture its knowledge in written form? Most top organizations accomplish this in the form of policies, work instructions and forms for example. A policy outlines why we do something. The 'why' is typically tied to an industry or regulatory requirement.

A work instruction is simply a procedure. This outlines a step-by-step process of how to do something in a respective work area. Other written knowledge may take the form of quick guides that assist leaders and staff in accomplishing tasks for a certain role. Irrespectively, every organization will need a process to capture its knowledge in order to create an environment of standard work.

The fourth critical factor of organizational knowledge is technology. Technology may take the form of online training modules or a knowledge management system. The knowledge management system needs to encompass as much organizational knowledge as possible and have certain attributes. The attributes center around capturing, storing, updating and sharing knowledge to the organization's talent. The key here is to ensure knowledge is current, relevant and accessible by all stakeholders.

Global Knowledge Process

Enterprise leaders will also need a global knowledge process to succeed in high-risk environments. The process should be simple, easily grasped by stakeholders and visually displayed. See Figure 5.2 for details. The first step in

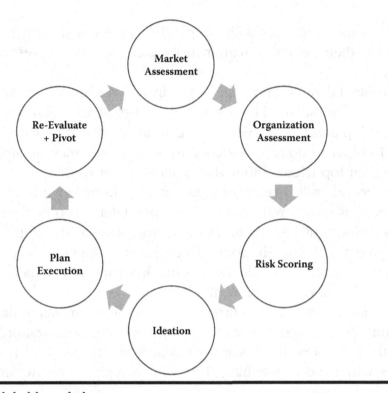

Figure 5.2 Global knowledge process.

the global process is a market assessment. This assessment is laser focused on determining the market's demand, supply and trends for knowledge.

The market focus may include an assessment of talent pools. Here there are several considerations for organizations to attract needed talent for critical roles. These pools may include academic programs, the current organization, other organizations and even other industries. The takeaway is that there are internal and external talent pools.

Let's use a nurse for example. There has been a nursing shortage in healthcare for years and this phenomenon does not appear to be slowing. If an organization needs nursing talent, they can seek these resources in the local or regional nursing programs. Some healthcare organizations even seek talent internationally and have achieved great success doing so by partnering with foreign academic programs.

Other talent pools could be internal to the organization. Are there employees who can be re-trained or upskilled in various areas to function as nurses if that is the talent of choice? Are there nurses working in support services areas who are not currently using their clinical skills? If so, can they be refreshed (skill wise) and deployed for help with staffing vacancies?

Leaders may also leverage talent pools from competitors. Industry speaking, this can be referred to as talent cannibalization where one organization takes talent from a competitor. Compensation and other perks tend to drive these opportunities and migration of talent between like organizations that are not affiliated. The takeaway is that the market assessment helps leaders understand what knowledge is available, needed and in high demand. Otherwise, organizations will essentially be driving blind and not know a crisis is approaching until arrives which is too late.

The next phase of the global knowledge process is an organizational assessment. Common considerations may include:

■ Where is the organizational knowledge currently concentrated?
■ Does the organization have a risk assessment tool to determine the level of risk to the organization for certain roles? If they become vacant, will a crisis ensue or will it be business as usual?
■ What percentage of the organization is retirement eligible?
■ What percentage of leadership is retirement age?
■ Are succession plans in place to mitigate these risks?
■ Do high-risk roles have a succession plan?
■ Does the organization have a formal knowledge transfer plan?
■ If not, why not?
■ What knowledge KPIs (key performance indicators) are being monitored?
■ Does the organization risk assess high-risk KPIs such as turnover, onboarding days (time to fill vacant roles), vacancy rates and the like?
■ Do respective leaders have real-time access to these data and is it being reviewed regularly?
■ Are critical events related to knowledge being reported to the governance and oversight leadership functions?
■ Is knowledge a part of the enterprise strategic planning process?

This is just a starter list of considerations. The point is leaders don't know what they don't know and can't fix a problem unless they know it's a problem. It's wise for organizations to consider frequent organizational knowledge assessments for strengths, gaps and risks.

Step three of the global knowledge process is risk scoring. It's imperative that leaders consider the risks for each phase of the knowledge process. There are several risk scoring tools that provide value in this process. Without an in-depth risk scoring process, leaders will essentially be driving blind.

Talent Canvas (Market View)

Let's take a closer look at Figure 5.3. Figure 5.3 represents a Talent Canvas from the market view.

Simply put, this concept looks outside the market and helps enterprise leaders assess risk for critical roles. Step one is to determine roles of interest. For example, the figure has a nurse, emergency manager and finance director. For each role, leaders will need to determine the market demand and market supply of each role.

Common considers per role include:

■ Is there a shortage of nurses currently?
■ Is there an abundance of emergency managers in the market?
■ Are finance Directors plentiful or non-existent in the market place?

The key here is to revert to basic micro economics. A shortage occurs when quantity demand is greater than quantity supplied. In contrast, a surplus exists when quantity supplied is greater than quantity demanded. If a shortage of workers exists, leaders must plan ahead as these high demand roles will more than likely be more expensive and take longer to fill.

Once the market demand and supply are determined, leaders should assign a risk level for each role. High risk equates to whether or not the role directly impacts life, safety and health. The next level of risk relates to if the role is critical to mission. The lowest level of risk means the role is important. But, does not pose an immediate risk to life, safety, health or mission if it becomes vacant.

Next, leaders should assign a total risk score and action priority level to each role. The total risk score is the sum of market demand, market supply and risk level as noted in Figure 5.3. The lower the total risk score indicates higher priority. Does the vacancy need an immediate, escalated or routine response if it becomes vacant? The total risk score helps guide the decision.

Let's briefly review this process for the nurse role. In Figure 5.3, nurses are in high demand and short supply. This indicates a shortage. Thus, leaders should expect to pay more for these roles. These roles are also high risk meaning they directly impact life, health and safety. So, the nurse role requires an immediate response from leaders to ensure gaps are filled quickly and prevented if at all possible.

Role	Market Demand	Market Supply	Role Risk Level (Impact if Role is Vacant)	Total Risk Score (Lower Score = Higher Priority)	Priority • Immediate Response • Escalated Response • Routine Response
Nurse	1	1	1	3	Immediate Response
Emergency Manager	2	2	2	6	Escalated Response
Finance Director	3	2	3	8	Routine Response

Market Demand Levels
• 1-High
• 2-Medium
• 3-Low

Market Supply Levels
• 1-Low
• 2-Medium
• 3-High

Role Risk Levels
• 1-Immediate Threat to Life, Safety, Health
• 2-Critical to Mission
• 3-Important, but not a threat to Life, Safety, Health or Mission

Figure 5.3 Talent canvas market view.

Talent Canvas (Organizational View)

Another tool that is very helpful for leaders in the knowledge risk assessment process is the Talent Canvas for the organizational view. See Figure 5.4 for details. This talent canvas focuses on the organization's internal knowledge current state. As noted in Figure 5.4, leaders again start by listing the desired roles or areas.

If C-Suite is a focal point, leaders would need to determine the total number of executives on the top leadership team. Then, determine what percentage of the team had less than 15 years tenure, between 15 and 25 years tenure and those with more than 25 years tenure. Also, it would be valuable to know what percentage of these leaders are at or beyond retirement age or seniority. Once these percentages are assigned, a priority score is given to each role, category of roles or area based on the risk potential.

The key here is to consider several points:

■ Where is the organization's knowledge for specific roles or areas?
■ What's the risk these roles will become vacant based on natural attrition?
■ Which roles or areas need to be a high priority for strategic and knowledge planning?

Let's look at Figure 5.4 practically. Seventy-five percent of the organization's top leaders have more than 25 years of tenure and are at or beyond retirement age. Thus, these roles are high risk for vacancy. Knowledge leaders would then need to ensure succession planning, knowledge sharing and depth in roles are aligned in case these roles became vacant. If not, these very important knowledge vessels could suddenly exit the organization, take their knowledge with them and a crisis would ensue.

Talent Risk Assessment Tool

A third tool to assist leaders in risk assessing organizational knowledge is noted in Figure 5.5. The Talent Risk Assessment Tool has several attributes. First, leaders identify roles of importance to the organization's knowledge plan. Then, score each role based on the impact it has on the scope of business. This score would be high, medium or low.

Next, leaders score each role for its focus area. Is the role a required function that the organization must have to provide basic services or products? Is the role a support function? In healthcare, for example, support

Role or Area	% of Roles with < 15 Years Tenure	% of Roles with 15-25 Years Tenure	% of Roles with > 25 Years Tenure	% of Roles at or beyond Retirement Age/Seniority	Priority 1. High (>50% Retirement Age or >50% at <15 Years Tenure) 2. Low (<50% Retirement Age or <50% at <15 Years Tenure)
Nursing AVPs	10%	20%	70%	70%	1
C-Suite	10%	15%	75%	75%	1
Directors	75%	25%	0%	0%	1
Managers	25%	50%	25%	25%	2

Figure 5.4   Talent canvas organizational view.

Role	Impact On the Organization Scope	Focus Area of Role	Depth of Role 1. No Primary or Backup Person 2. Primary Person 3. Primary + Backup Person	Risk Score (If Role is Vacant)	Total Risk Score (Lower Score = Higher Priority)	Priority • Immediate Response • Escalated Response • Routine Response
Chief Nursing Officer	1	1	1	1	4	Immediate Response
Chief Operating Officer	1	2	1	2	6	Escalated Response
Emergency Manager	2	2	3	2	9	Routine Response

Impact Scope Levels
- 1-High
- 2-Medium
- 3-Low

Focus Area Levels
- 1-Required Function
- 2-Support Function
- 3-Not required, but important for mission

Focus Levels
- 1-Required Function
- 2-Support Function
- 3-Not required, but important for mission

Risk Score Levels
- 1-Immediate Threat to Life, Safety, Health
- 2-Critical to Mission
- 3-Important, but not a threat to Life, Safety, Health or Mission

Figure 5.5   Talent risk assessment tool.

functions may include quality, accreditation, facilities management, environmental services and the like. They essentially support the enterprise functions to ensure continuity of services, but more times than not are not the main service function tied to core business.

Leaders should then consider if each role has proper depth. Is there a primary person assigned to the role? What about a backup person for each role which would provide two levels of depth? Does the role have neither a primary nor back up person? This would indicate a vacant role.

The next step is to risk score each individual role. This score simply determines the level of risk to the organization for each role. Does the role directly impact life, safety and health? Is the role critical to mission? Is the role important, but not a direct threat to life, safety, health or mission?

Then, the total risk score is calculated by adding columns 2–5 in Figure 5.5. The lower the score, the higher the risk and subsequent priority. Leaders must prioritize each role for a response. Lowest risk score should be first priority.

Let's take a look at a practical example. The Chief Nursing Officer role is a very critical role for a hospital to provide its bread and butter: clinical services. As noted in Figure 5.5, this role has high impact on the organization's scope of business. It's also a required function for the business to operate. Moreover, the current role is vacant which will directly impact life, safety and health. Thus, an immediate response is required to fill this role for continuity of services.

Global Knowledge Assessment Tool

A final tool to help enterprise leaders on the knowledge journey is noted in Figure 5.6. The Global Knowledge Assessment is the 30,000-foot view for top organizational leaders. There are many aspects of a strategic knowledge plan. But Figure 5.6 only notes a few for consideration.

First, enterprise leaders should determine which attributes comprise the organization's knowledge plan. These may include items such as succession planning, turnover, cross training, paired work assignments and a knowledge management system. Succession planning simply helps create a pipeline for critical roles. As previously mentioned, this correlates to depth in roles. Does each critical role have a primary and back person or two levels of depth? If not, further consideration is warranted.

Turnover is a big knowledge consideration. Over the years, we have learned that excessive and recurrent turnover can have dramatic effects on organization quality, service and cost. For example, one organization realized

Knowledge Attribute	Category 1. Foundational 2. Structural 3. Advanced	Goal	% of Organization with this Attribute	Gap	Rank 1. High Priority (>50% Gap) 2. Medium Priority (30%–50% Gap) 3. Low Priority (<30% Gap)
Succession Planning	1	80%	50%	30%	2
Turnover	1	80%	20%	60%	1
Cross Training	2	80%	45%	35%	2
Paired Work	2	80%	65%	15%	3
Knowledge Management System	3	80%	100%	0%	3

Figure 5.6   Global knowledge assessment.

turnover in one critical area was costing over $20 million per year during deep dive risk assessment. Many times, high turnover creates a culture wash and subsequent negative impact on value provided to customers.

Leaders should also consider attributes related to knowledge sharing. Does the organization have programs for cross training critical roles, paired assignments for less experienced leaders with more experienced counterparts and the like? It's imperative that organizations have a plan to share knowledge from person to person, across divisions and enterprise wide. Otherwise, gaps will emerge sooner than later.

Once knowledge attributes are determined, leaders categorize each attribute as foundational, structural or advanced. Think of building a house. The foundation comes first, then the walls (i.e., structure) are built. Finally, the fancy tile or hard wood floors are installed. These represent the advanced functions operationally speaking.

For each attribute, enterprise leaders need to assign a desired goal. Should 80% of the organization actively participate in each knowledge attribute for example? The goal will depend upon the enterprise knowledge strategy, scope and available resources. Next, each attribute is assessed for its presence across the enterprise and compared to the desired goal. The difference between the goal and percent of the organization implementing each attribute is the gap as noted in Figure 5.6. Finally, each attribute is assigned a rank or priority level.

Let's take a closer look at a simple example. In Figure 5.6, succession planning is a desired knowledge attribute of the enterprise leaders. This has been ranked as a foundational attribute that is required for the business to run effectively. The goal is to have a succession plan for at minimum 80% of the enterprise. Currently, only 50% of the organization has a succession plan. The gap is 30%. Thus, succession planning is ranked as a medium priority on the list based on the gap score as noted in the figure.

In contrast, turnover paints a much different picture. This too is a foundational attribute for the organization to function. The enterprise leaders feel at minimum 80% of the organization should be meeting the goal of less than 10% turnover annually. Currently, only 20% of the organization is meeting this goal. Thus, a 60% gap exists for this attribute. The end result is that turnover is a high priority for leaders.

Step three in the global knowledge process is ideation. This phase is an opportunity for enterprise leaders to review the assessments and risk scoring for the creation of plans to address gaps. In short, leaders should improve what is working and fix what is not working. Ideation is a team approach to developing new ideas, brainstorming and developing different perspectives to improve organizational knowledge.

The key here is team. It's imperative that enterprise leaders involve the right stakeholders in the process. Otherwise, they may fall prey to group think or a short-cited view of the knowledge spectrum. The art is to identify organizational blind spots that may have failed to appear on the radar previously.

The team should focus on aspects such as developing new pipelines or sources of talent. Transferring knowledge more effectively across the enterprise may also be a discussion point here. Other considerations could be internal training options to grow talent pools, innovative ways to repurpose old roles into new highly prized functions and filling any knowledge gaps that emerged during assessments. The end goal is to create an exhaustive list of options for expanding the organization's knowledge base.

Step four in the pursuit of knowledge mastery is executing the plan. The knowledge plan should coincide with the organization's strategic planning process. Execution should be timely, in sync with other organization priorities, funded properly and be a priority. Don't forget to assign a sponsor to the plan. The sponsor will ensure organizational knowledge becomes and remains a priority. Otherwise, knowledge will not grow, be cultivate or evolve with time.

Finally, the global knowledge process ends with re-evaluating and pivoting as needed. Frequently, leaders should reassess the market and organization's knowledge position. Frequency depends upon market speed and organizational agility. The market and various industries constantly change. Thus, so must the knowledge plan and its evolution. If gaps arise, enterprise leaders must pivot quickly, adjust the organization's knowledge trajectory and realign with the market. Otherwise, crisis will ensure and the lack of knowledge with unfavorably impact the organization's market position and long-term relevancy.

Summary

As noted, the new normal is change and the only constant. A byproduct of change is risk. The greater the organizational risk, the greater the response. Ignorance is not bliss in today's market. The more one knows, the better. Moreover, what leaders don't know can be a significant threat to organizational viability and success in long term.

The reality is that leaders and their organizations will need more than just basic knowledge to succeed in high-risk environments. It's imperative that thought leaders consider and master the critical factors of organizational knowledge. If knowledge gaps exist, the response should be laser focused, exact and timely. But, the aim will be off target if knowledge is not risk assessed each step of the way.

In summary, knowledge is a very powerful tool and a necessity in today's world. Without knowledge it's easy for people, organizations and leaders to perish (Hosea 4:6 KJV). The key is to ensure the organization's knowledge is stored in the proper vessels, shared continuously, readily available for stakeholders as needed and risk assessed.

Leaders simply don't know what they don't know. It's difficult if near impossible to solve a problem if leaders don't know one exists. Risk is the lock on the organizational success door. But, knowledge is the key that will open that door and ensure organizational success each and every time.

References

1. Merriam-Webster, 2021. https://www.merriam-webster.com/dictionary/risk
2. Merriam-Webster, 2021. https://www.merriam-webster.com/dictionary/knowledge

Chapter 6

Vision: The Cardinal Sin of Failing to Plan for Tomorrow by Focusing Solely on Today

Vision 2.0: Planning for the Road Ahead: Simple Tools Visionary Leaders Will Need to Succeed

The Value of Vision

Is vision required to succeed in high-risk environments? Is vision multi-dimensional or best seen through a single lens? Is vision an innate quality that all leaders possess or an attribute developed over time? Is perception always reality or will leaders need tools to properly discern truth from fiction? Is the vision of yesterday still relevant for tomorrow or is a pivot required? Is it possible for leaders to risk assess their future view? We will answer these and other considerations in the following.

Vision can be defined as, 'a thought, concept, or object formed by the imagination.'[1] This concept is synonymous with perception, discernment and foresight.[1] 'Where there is no vision, the people perish' (Proverbs 29:18 KJV). The key to crafting an organizational vision lies in the assessment of days past, current state and ideal future state.

The reality is that change is the new normal and only constant. Leaders must view the organization's road ahead through multiple lens. One of the biggest pitfalls is to have a silo approach to strategic planning. Vision is multi-dimensional in nature. Thus, the plan for the journey ahead must be multifocal.

DOI: 10.4324/9781003267966-6

Let's take a closer look at a few tools visionary leaders will need to succeed in high-risk market environments.

Market Journey Map

The first step in creating a transformational vision is considering a market journey map. See Figure 6.1 for details. The concept is essentially a quick review of where the market has been, where it is currently and where it appears to be going. All three views (past, present and future) are needed to complete a proper visionary assessment.

It's important to note, that Figure 6.1 is an example of the healthcare industry's journey over the last couple of decades. This is simply an example. The market journey map can and should be adjusted based on the market or industry focus. For the purposes of this discussion, the concept is more important than the content in Figure 6.1.

For years, the healthcare industry focused on local completion. This is the first tollgate in the market journey map. The industry perception was one focused on brick-and-mortar health services. This simply means that the leadership focus was to build physical care sites and locations. The adage, 'if you build it they will come,' was the theme for this period. If health services were needed, the customer would travel to a physical location to receive the desired care and services.

Operationally, leaders of the time were focused on meeting goals tied to service, cost and quality. The perception was 'if we can outperform our local competition,' then we win the market share. The key to this era of the industry was the local focus.

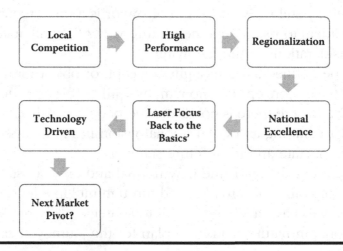

Figure 6.1   Market journey map.

The second tollgate along the industry's journey was high performance. The industry experienced a change in dynamic where operational leaders injected improvement concepts such as Lean, Six Sigma and the like. The whole premise or vision was to outperform the competition by improving the current state incrementally. The adage, 'better, faster, cheaper,' was the common theme in leadership circles. Thus, the industry experienced an influx of process engineers and improvement methodologies to assist organizational leaders in achieving this aim.

The third tollgate relates to regionalization. The healthcare industry started viewing the industry's future through smart growth, larger footprints and a regional approach to care. This simply means the local or stand-alone model faded quickly. Larger organizations began to grow and smaller organizations began to look for partners. The goal here was to find economies of scale, synergies and competitive advantage through growth and partnerships.

The fourth tollgate, as shown in Figure 6.1, landed on national excellence. The theme here was ensuring the organization was a national best practice site. The local and regional vision was replaced by the national scale based on excellence. Excellence was driven by crafting a vision to ensure the organization would be 'the' best site for care due to superior service, cost, quality, access and overall value. This tollgate was the catalyst for industry transformation and technology's preeminence began to emerge.

The fifth tollgate was a laser focus on being 'the' best and 'first' site for care. Organizations began honing their visions for the future by focusing on the basics. This era was marked by a shift in consumer presence and influence. Organizations heightened their strategies and visions for the future based on customer expectations, feedback and requests.

In short, leaders took a back seat to the customer. The customer began to drive the industry bus so to speak. Only those organization's that could master the basics and exceed customer requirements each and every time would live to see the road ahead. The main foci here were magnifying customer needs, efficiency, transparency with prices and adding value to each customer at every turn. At the end of the day, health services customers have choice and mobility. Thus, organizational leaders were forced to become more agile, change acceptant, learn and craft visions for the future radically different than those of yesteryears.

The sixth tollgate was evidenced by the magnification of technology. Instead of driving to a brick and mortar building for care, healthcare consumers now accessed care via smart technology. Innovation and new access channels became the common place. Consumers now used smart devices, the internet and video conferencing, for example, to connect with healthcare providers and receive care. The key here is that the customer's perspective radically transformed the way healthcare was planned, executed and evolved.

As noted in the figure, the next tollgate is to be determined. Thus, visionary leaders should take great care to predict the next step and ensure their organizations are properly positioned to thrive. One of the best indicators of future behavior is past behavior. Therefore, visionaries would presume that change would continue to disrupt the healthcare industry based on the market journey map. Simply put, tomorrow will be different than today and leaders must evolve into master change agents.

The takeaway is leaders often do not know what they do not know. A bird's eye view of past, present and expected future is a great starting point for vision planning. A journey map is a very simple, effective and needed tool to look forward based on the market's past.

Organizational Road Map

The second tool visionary leaders will need to succeed is an organizational roadmap. See Figure 6.2 for details. It's imperative that thought leaders mirror the market's journey and expected next pivot with this concept. The organizational roadmap is simply a future vision of next steps the organization must take to be successful long-term.

Common considerations may include:

■ What is the current state of the organization's journey?
■ Where are we now?
■ What is the expected next step we need to take based on market data?
■ Is the organization positioned to move ahead?
■ Are we headed in the right direction?
■ Does the organization have the right talent to move to the next tollgate?
■ Is the organization structured properly for the current environment?
■ What's the desired end and what steps are needed to get there?

These are just a few considerations for thought leaders to ponder when crafting the plan ahead.

As noted in Figure 6.2, the organizational road map will depend on the current market, the organization's structure, available resources and the expected road ahead. The key here is ensuring the road map will lead the enterprise to a successful end. It's simply a series of tollgates that will lead the

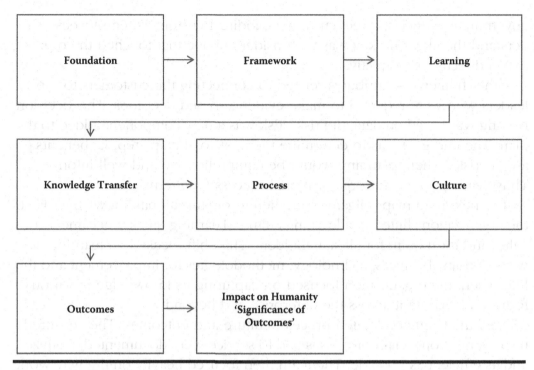

Figure 6.2 Organizational road map.

organization step by step to the desired operational plateau. The main goal is forward progress that is measurable, desired and controlled.

Figure 6.2 is a simple road map example that a transformational team used to take a large service organization from average to high performance quickly. The market of the time demanded organizations operate more efficiently and effectively than ever before. Thus, attributes of value such as service, cost, quality, access and innovative technology were the new requirement.

They began the organizational journey with foundation building. This phase focused on the organization's structure, functions, value streams and the like. Think of the organizational chart, service portfolio and reporting structures. The key here was to reprogram the organization from a traditional, bulky, slow and manual-focused enterprise model, to one laden with speed, agility and technology. This tollgate was an organizational priority and impediment to step two.

The second tollgate for the organization's road map was creating an innovative framework. The framework tied several strategic pieces of the vision together. The core of the framework was establishing who the customers were and what they required. Prior to this, the customer list was meager. The new list was exhaustive and included stakeholders such as communities, government agencies, direct customers, indirect customers, employees, leaders and the like. The key was to consider anyone that touched the organization directly or indirectly.

Other framework attributes related to connecting the customers to top leaders who were required to make evidence-based decisions. This decision making was based on data and risk. Risk was a new component added to the plan. The end goal was to determine the next road map step, its benefits and its risks. Then, planning would be comprehensive and well informed. Thus, leading to greater organizational success long-term.

The next road map tollgates were tied to organizational knowledge. First, the organization shifted to a learning culture. Learning quickly became a core value and focal point for all stakeholders. This shift focused on learning new ways of doing business, technology, methodologies for improvement and the like. Then, the organization focused on capturing its knowledge in various forms and sharing it across the enterprise and beyond.

Next the team accelerated process, culture and outcomes. They ensured the organization's main processes tied to service were documented, analyzed and as efficient as possible. The team then focused heavily on the way work was done in the organization which leads to culture. The goal was to create a culture of standard work. This ensured everyone in the organization at each level did work correctly and the same way each time. Thus, eliminating variation and its disastrous effects.

These accomplishments lead to transformational outcomes that directly impacted humanity on many fronts. The plan for progression on the road map was simple. Push the organization to the next tollgate, measure everything to find the wins and publish what was significant (statistically speaking). The end game was significant service improvements that greatly impacted humanity (i.e., the customer base).

In summary the organizational road map is a tool that is simple, very effective and a great visual display of where the organization is going next. A huge part of success is creating a vision that the organization can see adds value, leads to the desired end and will positively impact everyone. A road map is a great fit for these needs.

Five-Year Plan

The next tool visionary leaders will need to succeed is the five-year strategic plan. See Figure 6.3 for details.

Focus Area	Year 1	Year 2	Year 3	Year 4	Year 5
Strategic Theme	*Foundation + Culture Transformation*	*High Performance*	*System Integration*	*Transformative System of Health*	*Magnification*
Service (HCAHPS)					
Financial • Revenue • Costs • Capital • EBITDA					
Quality • Mortality • Infections					
People • Engagement • Employee Satisfaction • Turnover • New Roles • Succession Planning					
Regulatory					
Smart Growth • Service Lines • Access Points • Geographic Footprint					
Efficiency					
Technology + Analytics (Digital Strategy)					

Figure 6.3 Five year plan.

This tool is more detailed than the road map. But, it's a simple crosswalk that helps the organization's leaders plan for the future. As noted in Figure 6.3, common focus areas are tied to what the organizations perceive to add value.

In healthcare, for example, five-year planning includes attributes such as:

■ customer satisfaction
■ financials (costs, revenue, profit, capital)
■ quality indicators
■ people scores
■ regulatory requirements
■ growth plans
■ efficiency
■ technology

The key to success with this tool is to keep it simple. What will the organization need to be successful each year ahead over the next five years? The desired end is forward progress and measurable improvements over time. The goals for each strategic focus area act as the rudder to steer the ship forward. Many organizations use national benchmarks for their goal setting. The end goal is for leaders to be able to see the organization's aim, realistic goals and what success really looks like in one document.

The Process

Once strategic planners have a good pulse check of past, present and future, they will need a process for planning, implementation and improvement. See Figure 6.4 for details.

The Vision 2.0 process begins with discovery. This process allows leaders to discover what is working and what is not working, organizationally speaking. For example, is the organization good with change but struggles with sustaining wins? There are many scenarios to consider. The takeaway is for the first step to involve learning so the road map ahead is and stays on the right track.

Step two, the process is ideation. This simply occurs when various stakeholders think and plan together. The goal here is to avoid group think and other biases that hamper new ways of doing business. New ideas, technology, best practices and the like are common discussion points. The desired end is to create the best canvas for the road ahead that ensures success.

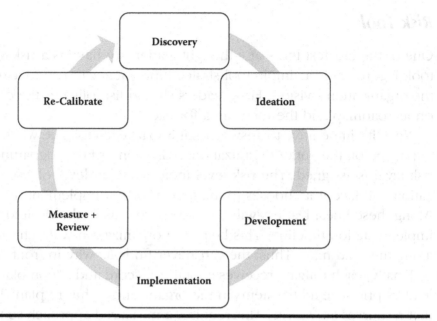

Figure 6.4 Strategic process.

Step three of the process is plan development. Strategic plans should be structured, well thought out, consistent, aligned with market direction and executed flawlessly. The biggest pitfall leaders face in planning is not understanding organizational strengths, gaps and risks. The ideal is to craft a future plan for the organization that is aggressive enough to push everyone forward without pushing too fast to quickly and subsequently leaving critical stakeholders behind.

The next several steps of future planning are implementing the plan, measuring progress and re-calibrating as needed. The key focus here is to ensure the organization has a cadence for the future. What's coming should never catch leaders or staff off guard. If vision planning is done correctly, the enterprise in most cases should be prepared for and be able to handle the changes.

Once plans for the future are implemented, leaders must measure the organization's forward progress. Simply put, a good indicator is goal attainment tied to the targets on the organization's five-year plan. If goal attainment is adequate and tollgates are being achieved, then keep going. If not, strategic leaders should take a step back, recalibrate and try a different direction. Otherwise, it's just doing something for the sake of doing it versus adding value.

Risk Tool

One of the greatest tools any thought leader can have is a risk assessment tool. Figure 6.5 is a simple tool strategic planners can use to assess risks for the organization's vision. First, leaders should list tollgates the enterprise has on its roadmap and the focus area for each.

Next, it's imperative to answer what impact each tollgate will have. Will the impact be on the entire organization, a division or just a department? Then, a risk level is assigned. The risk level indicates what level of risk the organization will face if it chooses to implement or not implement the next step. Along these lines, leaders will score each step as to the desired or actual implementation timeline. This helps the organization walk chronologically along the road map. Thus, the cart never finds its way in front of the horse.

Finally, each tollgate receives a total risk score and action plan. This helps leaders prioritize all the items in the organization's future plan. The reality is that resources are scarce. This requires a measured approach so there will be enough gas in the tank to get the organization to the finish line. Moreover, the highest risk items should receive first priority.

Let's look a real example. In Figure 6.5, the first tollgate for consideration is establishing an innovation hub. The focus for the program would be to develop new ideas, way of doing business and technology for a competitive advantage. This new program would impact the entire enterprise and its stakeholders.

Also, the risk level and expected benefits are relatively low. The implementation time is less than three years. Because of the scorings, the total risk score would be 9 as noted in Figure 6.5. When comparing all the tollgates on the list, the leaders would give this one last priority based on its risk score.

The key here is for leaders to assess, prioritize and leverage risks effectively. Not every initiative will need the same organizational response. Here the end goal is to ensure leaders are focusing on what is important and not wasting scarce resources.

Review Cycle

The final tool thought leaders need is a review cycle. In markets where change is scarce, review cycles can be extended. In contrast, when markets are turbulent and riddled with chronic disruptions leaders and their organizations must review the organization's progress more frequently. In today's world, change is the new norm. Thus, organizational review timelines

Tollgate	Focus Area	Impact Scope	Risk Level (If we do or do not adopt the Tollgate)	Benefit Rating	Implementation Time (Years)	Total Risk Score • Add Scores: Impact Scope + Risk Level + Benefit Rating • Lower Scores = Highest Priority	Action • Execute Now • Execute Within 1 Year • Table to Next Cycle
Establish Innovation Hub	Innovation	1	3	3	2	9	Table to Next Cycle
Add Service Line	Revenue	2	2	2	1	7	Execute Within 1 Year
Build New Hospital	Access to Services	1	1	1	2	5	Execute Now
Merger with Larger Organization	Growth	1	2	2	3	8	Execute Within 1 Year

Impact Scope
1. Enterprise Wide Impact
2. Entity or Divisional Impact
3. Department Impact

Risk Level
1. Risk to life, health or safety
2. Risk to Mission
3. Important, but not a risk to life, health, safety or Mission

Benefit Rating
1. Immediate Benefit to life, health or safety
2. Immediate Benefit to Mission
3. Important, but not an Immediate Benefit to life, health, safety or Mission

Implementation Timeline
1. < 1 Year
2. 1-3 Years
3. 3-5 Years
4. > 5 Years

Figure 6.5 Risk tool.

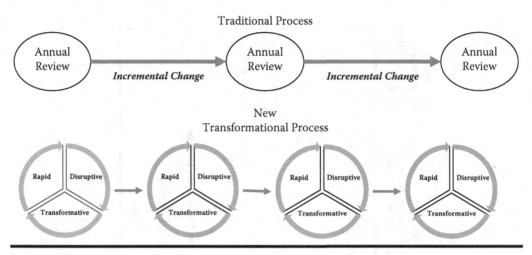

Figure 6.6 Review cycle.

must be conducted very frequently. Otherwise, the market will leave the enterprise behind.

See Figure 6.6 for details. Traditionally, it was acceptable to review strategic plans and subsequent progress annually. The key here is over five-year period, for example, there would only be five reviews with incremental changes in between. The adage 'hurry up and slow down' applies here.

In contrast, the new transformational process exhibits cycles of fast, disruptive and radically different action plans. The key here is frequency and action. These reviews may be conducted as often as each month, market dependent. Soon following would be pivots or change that is rapid and disrupts the current state. If the market is disruptive, so must be the planning review process and associated outcomes.

Summary

The old is gone and the new is here. Today's market is now dictating a high-risk change environment. The greater the change, the greater levels of risk organizations must consider. The takeaway is that leaders must have vision to succeed in high-risk environments. Also, vision cannot be viewed in a one-dimensional lens.

The market is multi-dimensional and so must be the future plans to succeed. The reality is that vision is not always an innate quality that all leaders possess. It must be developed over time. Thus, leaders will need tools to properly discern truth from fiction and perception from reality.

There is one sure bet for the road ahead. It will be different from today. The only question is how many leaders will craft a new lens to see the future. Future plans of yesterday will only remain viable for tomorrow if they are nimble, agile and measured frequently for success. Leaders simply don't know what they don't know. The key for clarity is vision plans, road maps, risk tools and evidence-based decision making.

Reference

1. Merriam-Webster, 2021. https://www.merriam-webster.com/dictionary/vision

Chapter 7

Conflict: The Cardinal Sin of Mismanaging Relationships to Drive Outcomes

The Art of Conflict Resolution: What Leaders Must Know to Thrive in a Change-Driven Market

Conflict & Its Importance

In today's world, change is the new normal and only constant. With change, conflict is guaranteed to follow in some form or fashion as the operating norm is disrupted. The only question is how will leaders respond? Will the leadership response invoke the desired resolution or simply make the problem worse?

This topic worths several considerations. Is all conflict negative? Will conflict evoke both positive and negative organizational responses? Should leaders respond to all conflicts the same way or is discernment needed? Do all conflicts pose the same risk to the organization and its stakeholders? Is a formal process needed to help guide leaders through conflict or can they simply wing it?

A conflict is, 'the opposition of persons or forces that give rise to the dramatic action.'[1] In layman's terms, conflict occurs when parties find a difference that conflicts with their respective world views. The reason that conflict is so important or relevant to leadership is because we will all face it

DOI: 10.4324/9781003267966-7

at various stages along the career journey. Thus, leaders must be prepared to respond, engage and resolve conflicts both proactively and reactively.

The desired end to conflict is finding some form of resolution. Conflict resolution can be defined as, 'the informal or formal process that two or more parties use to find a peaceful solution to their dispute.'[2] As change has become, how leaders respond to conflict must evolve as well. But, how will leaders respond appropriately unless they truly understand this topic? In short, they won't.

Levels of Conflict

For the sake of this discussion, there are several levels of conflict worth noting. See Figure 7.1 for details. The first level of conflict resolution relates to interpersonal conflict. This level can be as simple as two individuals who disagree on a topic or present a formal grievance to leadership over a dispute. Technically speaking, these lower level issues often tend to be less impactful to the organization and easier to address.

The next level is departmental conflict. This typically occurs when the conflict affects a department consisting of a group of people. A simple example could be a group of a hundred employees in a single department who are divided over a newly implemented uniform policy. Again, as the level of conflict grows so do the number of stakeholders affected. Thus, leaders must be very mindful of the response and subsequent resolution.

The third level of conflict resolution relates to a divisional or programmatic conflict. This occurs when several departments in a division or an entire program that may affect large sections of the enterprise are at odds over an issue. The higher the level of conflict, the greater concern for leaders and the

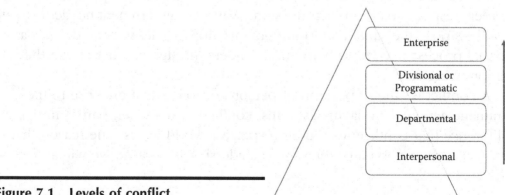

Figure 7.1   Levels of conflict.

governance body. An example of programmatic conflict could occur during an organizational merger for example. The point(s) of contention would be whose leadership would control the program and lead its future direction. There are many examples here, but this is just one simple one.

The final and most impactful level of conflict relates to the enterprise as a whole. This level of conflict tends to impact all organizational stakeholders. Dependent upon the organization's scope, this could include thousands of interested parties. These stakeholders include but are not limited to staff, leaders, communities, government bodies, accrediting organizations and many others.

The key here is that this level of conflict will typically impact everyone who touches the organization internally and externally. A good example would be a large competitor that enters the local market of a service organization and threatens to take 50% or more of the service due to superior quality, service and costs. Here top organizational leaders will need to act decisively, quickly and with laser focus to save the organization's revenue to stream and ensure long-term market relevancy. The key here is that everyone in the organization will be impacted by this level of conflict in one way or the other. Thus, the response must be globally crafted to ensure all stakeholders are properly represented.

The Conflict Resolution Process

For leaders to succeed, they need a good process. See Figure 7.2 for details. There are many ways to address conflict, and leaders should first ensure they

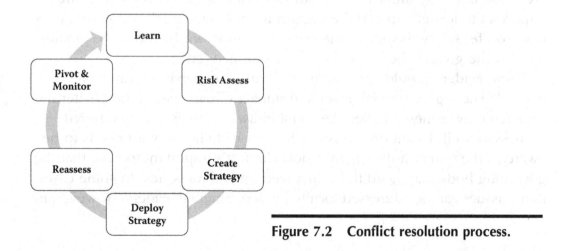

Figure 7.2 Conflict resolution process.

adhere to organizational, local and federal guidelines for conflict resolution. However, Figure 7.2 provides a good starting point for consideration.

Step one is to learn as much as possible about the situation. There are several questions to consider:

- What is the issue?
- Why is it an issue?
- Who does it impact?
- How far does the conflict reach?
- What is the risk to the organization and its stakeholders?
- What are the risks if the conflict is ignored?
- What are the risks if the conflict is addressed?
- What benefits are expected from conflict resolution?

Step two, leaders must risk assess each conflict. It's important to understand what risk is present, its scope and to craft an appropriate leadership response. See Figure 7.3 for details. A simple risk assessment tool begins by listing the issue(s). This is imperative for a visual display so issues make it to the leadership radar and stay there until resolved.

Next, each issue should be assessed for its scope. Is the issue departmental, divisional or enterprise wide? The scope of the issue will directly and significantly impact the organization's response. The greater the scope or impact, the greater the leadership priority and response to the issue.

Once scope is determined, leaders must determine the level of risk each issue poses to the enterprise. As noted in Figure 7.3, level 1 risks are those that directly impact life, safety or health of its stakeholders. Level 2 risks are those that may impact the organization's mission. Level 3 risks are important to leadership and the organization. However, they are not direct risks to life, safety, health or the enterprise mission. In short, the greater the risk the greater the leadership response needed.

Then, leaders should determine the level of leadership awareness needed. The higher the risk level and impact of each issue, the greater the leadership awareness needed. Leadership awareness is a simple tiered process as well. Based on the issue, leaders will choose who needs to be aware of the issue on the organization chart. It's important to note that the governing body may need to be involved on certain issues. In some cases, minor issues can be addressed locally by departmental leaders. However, in

Issue (Type of Conflict)	Scope Score	Risk Level	Leadership Awareness Level	Total Risk Score • Add Scores: Scope + Risk Level + Leadership Awareness Level • Lower Scores = Higher Priority	Leadership Priority • Routine Response • Escalated Response • Emergent Response
Employee to Employee Grievance	3	3	3	9	Routine Response
Regional Competitor Encroaches by winning Service Contract that threatens the organization's revenue	1	2	1	4	Escalated Response
Organizational Merger-conflict between leadership over operational control of a critical program	1	1	1	3	Emergent Response

Risk Level
1. Risk to life, health or safety
2. Risk to Mission
3. Important, but not a risk to life, health, safety or Mission

Scope
1. Enterprise Wide Impact
2. Entity or Divisional Impact
3. Department Impact

Leadership Awareness Level
1. Top Leadership + Governing Body
2. Top Leadership
3. Local Leadership (Divisional and/or Department Leaders)

Figure 7.3 Conflict risk assessment tool.

extreme cases top leaders and the governing body must be aware of and directly involved with addressing the risk.

Next, leaders should assign a total risk score to each issue as noted in Figure 7.3. The key here is that lower scores are higher priority. Thus, require a greater response from leadership. Let's take a look at a few practical examples noted in Figure 7.3.

As noted in the figure, an organization has three conflicts to address. These challenges consist of an employee grievance, new market competitor threatening its service area and a merger with a larger organization creating conflict between program leaders. For the employee grievance, the scope is departmental. This simply means that local department or divisional leaders can address the issue. The risk to the organization is important, but not a threat to life, safety, health or mission. Thus, a routine leadership response is indicated.

The new market competitor is a much bigger threat to the enterprise. This conflict will impact the entire organization and is not a direct threat to life, health and safety. Moreover, the risk requires both top leaders and the governing board to be aware of and actively involved in addressing this conflict. Thus, the total risk score indicates an escalated response from leadership.

The final example in Figure 7.3 is the organizational merger creating programmatic conflict between leadership. The conflict impacts the entire enterprise and poses immediate risk to life, health and safety. Also, it necessitates that top leaders including the governing body should need awareness and direct involvement in resolution efforts. This issue has the lowest total risk score. Thus, leaders must consider an emergent response.

The key with the conflict resolution risk assessment tool is for all issues to be captured, risk assessed and addressed appropriately. Not every conflict will require the same response. Leaders have limited time, resources and bandwidth. Thus, they will have to prioritize conflict and subsequent solutions to be effective in this arena.

Step three of conflict resolution as noted in Figure 7.2 is crafting and implementing a strategy. A simple tool for this step in the process is the conflict resolution canvas. Here the key is to visually display the perspectives of each affected party. The end goal is to determine what is success for adequate resolution to the conflict. A significant part of the process is to determine what each part must have, cannot have and would like to have. The middle ground essentially is the catalyst to the conflict resolution strategy.

Let's take a closer look at the example in Figure 7.4. Two organizations are in the process of merging similar business units. Each business has a large geographic service area and hundreds of employees. Party 1 perceives success to be achieved if both parties combine into one brand, have consolidated operations and implement the merger within a year. In contrast, Party 2 believes success for the merger is predicated on achieving operational cost savings, improved services and a three-month implementation timeframe.

Both sides finally landed on the middle ground to formulate a successful strategy to resolve the conflicts. This 'happy medium' was achieved by both parties agreeing to a hybrid organizational brand fairly representing both entities, a focus on improving services and an eight-month implementation timeframe. The key is understanding what each party deems as success and finding the 'happy medium.'

Next, the parties used the canvas for the other attributes. In short, Party 1 felt the merged organization had to have local control of operations and their leader in charge of the new business. In contrast, Party 2 expected shared leadership and representative leaders from both sides running the new brand. The middle ground was an agreement of local control that was shared by both entities.

The parties then used the canvas to outline deal breakers. Party 1 could not agree to a deal that would produce revenue loss, cost increases or a lack of leadership representation. In contrast, Party 2's deal breakers were essentially the same as noted in Figure 7.4. The key middle ground was to create a combined leadership structure where both organizations were represented equally and focused on financial efficiencies.

Finally, the canvas was used to outline what each entity would like to have. As noted in Figure 7.4, there were similarities and differences. However, the parties used this simple tool to visually display their perspectives, needs, interests and desired end. The art was crafting the middle ground or strategy to resolve the conflict and move to a successful middle ground.

The final steps in the conflict resolution process are reassessment, pivots and monitoring. It's imperative for leaders to measure the process and its outcomes to predetermined goals. Otherwise, who will one know when success is achieved or missed? Equally important is for leaders to reassess progress to ensure wins are maintained and improved upon. If slippage is noted, change leaders must pivot and find a new solution to ensure forward

Considerations	Party1 Inputs	Middle Ground	Party2 Inputs
What is Success?	• 1 Organizational Brand • Combined Operations • Improved & More Efficient Services • 1 year Implementation Timeline	• Hybrid Organizational Brand Representing Both Organizations • Improved & More Efficient Services • 8 Month Implementation Timeline	• Cost Savings • Improved & More Efficient Services • 3 Month Implementation timeline
Must Haves	• Local Control of Operations • Current Leader the Dominant Leader in the Merged Organization	• Combined Leadership Structure • Local Control of Operations	• Representative Leadership of Both Pre-Merger Organizations
Can't Haves (Deal Breakers)	• Revenue Loss • Cost Increases • Lack of Leadership Representation of both Organizations	• Combined Leadership Structure with Representation from Organizations	• Lack of Leadership Representation of Both Organizations • Cost Increases
Like to Haves	• Operational Control of the Merged Business • Increased Revenue Post Merger • Dominant Ownership Stake of Merged Organization		• Operational Control of the Merged Business • Increased Revenue Post Merger • Equal Ownership Stake of Merged Organization

Figure 7.4 Conflict resolution tool.

progress. Finally, leaders must continuously monitor conflict issue both short term and long term. As previously noted, change is the new norm. If the market and stakeholder expectations are constantly evolving, so must the strategies leaders use to resolve conflicts.

Conflict Resolution Roles

The final key to successful conflict resolution, for leaders, is to understand, grasp and effectively leverage various roles. See Figure 7.5 for details. In Figure 7.5, there are several roles in the conflict resolution process. These roles are representative and not exhaustive.

First, conflict most always originates with an instigator or aggressor. This role typically initiates conflict with some desired end in mind. Aggressors may see a personal or professional benefit from engaging in conflict. For example, if organizations merge and leaders feel threatened. One response may be for one or more leaders to attempt to marginalize their counterparts so they retain their current role or gain a promotion in the new organization. The key here is for leaders to respond correctly.

As noted in Figure 7.5, leaders must handle aggressors carefully. Common responses could be to first learn as much as possible about each participant's view point, expectations, needs and desired end. Next, leaders may choose to de-escalate the aggressor's behavior using various techniques or marginalize them so their impact on the organization is limited. The key here is the risk assessment as previously noted. The level of risk and impact of the aggressor's actions will correlate directly to the leader's response. Each situation is different. Thus, responses will vary.

Role	Attribute(s)	Leader Response Options
Instigator or Aggressor	Initiates the conflict	Learn; Risk Assess; De-escalate; Marginalize; Resolve
Defender	Reacts to the Instigator	Learn; Risk Assess; Support; Defend; Remove; Resolve
Bystander	Observes the conflict	Learn; Risk Assess; Remove
Enabler	Contributes to the conflict	Learn; Risk Assess; De-escalate; Marginalize; Remove

Figure 7.5   Conflict resolution roles.

The second role relates to the defender. In conflict resolution, defenders are those that tend to react to the instigators or aggressors. Situation dependent, defenders typically are those who receive the brunt of the conflict. Irrespectively, leaders will have to learn about the defenders first. Then, craft a strategy to resolve the conflict. Techniques of choice for resolution may include supporting, defending or removing the defender from the conflict. Again, the risk assessment will dictate the response. However, the goal for leaders is to reach a middle ground with the least collateral damage possible.

The third role in conflict resolution is the bystander. Bystanders are synonymous with onlookers. They typically are third parties who watch the conflict from a distance, but can be impacted directly or indirectly situation dependent. The key here is, for leaders, to learn, risk assess and remove the bystanders from the conflict situation.

The final conflict role is the enabler. This role typically contributes to the conflict. The adage 'adding fuel to the fire' applies here. Dependent upon the issue, enablers may positively or negatively impact the situation. Again, leaders must quickly learn as much about this actor type and risk assess their impact on the conflict. Then, implement a strategy of sorts that may include de-escalation, marginalization or removing the enablers from the situation.

The end goal is to know who the actors in conflict resolution are, what impact they have or can have and craft a strategy to magnify the good and marginalize the bad.

Summary

As previously noted, in today's world change is the new norm and only constant. An expected byproduct of change is conflict. Whether the conflict is between two people, a division or competing organizations, leaders must understand the environment to craft the appropriate response. Conflict varies in nature and source. Thus, so must the resolution(s).

It's also important to note that some conflict is short-lived, recurrent or cyclical and other issues are long-term. Moreover, conflict can arise from various sources. Sources include but may not be limited to a fear response from people, a perceived gain in money, power or position and unfortunately sometimes due to pride. One of the most predominant sources of conflict relates to culture. Culture clashes are extremely disruptive, toxic and dangerous for leaders and their organizations. At all costs, leaders must prevent, plan for and quickly mitigate cultural disruptions or conflict that will definitely arise.

In summary, all conflict is not negative. Some conflict such as competition among competing organizations has positive out shoots. These may include increased investment in research and development, creation of innovative technologies and more efficient ways of operating. The key is to look for the bright spot in every conflict.

Also, all conflict is not the same. Thus, leaders must craft responses and strategies to fit each individual conflict. The risk assessment tool is invaluable in this process. Otherwise, the aim will be off target, leaders will become ineffective and the organization will experience undesired consequences of conflict. The key is that the means must lead to the desired end of successful conflict resolution.

Finally, leaders must master the art of learning. Keys here are knowing: What's the issue, its risk, its scope and the actors that affect success or failure? In today's world, ignorance is not bliss. What leaders don't know will definitely impact the final outcome. Thus, leaders must craft a conflict resolution process, stick to it and evolve with time. The end goal for leaders is to ensure they master and conquer conflict resolution before it conquers them.

References

1. Merriam-Webster, 2021. https://www.merriam-webster.com/dictionary/conflict
2. Harvard Law School, 2020. https://www.pon.harvard.edu/daily/conflict-resolution/what-is-conflict-resolution-and-how-does-it-work/

The Snapback Effect: When Culture Misaligns with Process Change

Introduction

One of the biggest challenges leaders face in disruptive markets is getting change to stick. The million-dollar question is why? Change occurs when leaders 'give a different position, course, or direction to'[1] an aspect of the business. Change is the new norm and the only constant in today's world.

Unfortunately, there is no sign that the disruptive changes we have experienced in the last few years, particularly in healthcare, are slowing down anytime soon.

Recently, a large service organization began to experience higher than normal levels of disruption related to safety and quality of services. The challenges were significant enough in one large business unit to garner the attention of senior leaders for the enterprise as the outcomes became an immediate risk to life, safety and well-being of its customers. Consequently, the senior leader overseeing this operation assigned a change agent (i.e., black belt) to this business unit to quell the storm. This was the organizational trend and the most common knee-jerk reaction when crises arose, operationally speaking.

The change agent was thrust into the business unit with little insight as to why so much disruption was occurring. The business unit was directly responsible for providing necessary services to thousands of customers in the region. Without access to these services, many customers would suffer, experience unfavorable health outcomes and even worse in critical scenarios. The initiative began with a simple assessment to gauge the degree of risk for the organization and its customers. The ultimate goal was to create a road map to quell the storm, eliminate the safety and quality issues and prevent the storm from reoccurring in the future.

An initial assessment revealed some very interesting results. The change agent went immediately to the base of the fire operationally speaking. The first step was a series of onsite meetings with the business unit's leaders for a better understanding of the issues, their context and degree of risk to all stakeholders. During these initial sessions, many leaders assigned blame for the crisis on various attributes such as compensation, turnover, high vacancy rates, limited budgets and the like.

The conversations evolved into several sessions of rounding to engage those on the front lines. Simply put, the team conducted Gemba walks where the work was actually occurring. The change agent immediately noticed some obvious contributors. In some areas of the business unit, it was obvious top leadership did not round on a regular basis if ever. There was an obvious disconnect between the top leader and the front-line workers during the rounding sessions. Just a side note. It's exceedingly difficult for leaders to solve problems, if they are grossly disconnected to the work and those doing the work.

The Gemba walks also revealed areas that were in gross ill repair due to simple negligence. The resources were available for simple housekeeping and standardization, but not deployed. The question is, why? Unfortunately, these and other simple operational attributes directly impacted thousands of customers unfavorably.

To complement the Gemba walks, the change agent conducted a very simple high-level data analysis that was also very interesting. The data revealed that the quality and safety issues did not just begin. The business unit had experienced declines in quality and safety scores for a several-year period. The operational declines initially were subtle, but gained momentum with time. Think of an avalanche racing down a mountain. At first the avalanche may be unnoticeable. However, as momentum gains one can see it from a mile away.

As a result, the analysis revealed a cyclical pattern. Every few months or so the business unit would experience a crisis of some sort. The leadership team would deploy change agents much like a fire brigade. The issues were quelled temporarily, but later resurfaced even worse than before. The real question needing to be answered was, why did these disruptive issues 'snapback' after being resolved?

Within a very short timeframe, the change agent realized quickly that more information was needed to correctly diagnose and solve the issues. Thus, a case study followed where the troubled business unit was compared in various ways to other higher performing units to segment perception from reality. Let's take a closer look.

Case Study

The change agent assembled a team and began the deep dive. The team compared the troubled business unit (Unit 1) to two higher performing business units (Units 2 and 3). See Figure 7.6 for details.

All business units were comparable in size, scope of services and customer bases. The attributes chosen for the study included turnover, improvement outcomes from projects, leadership attributes related to Black Belt training, goal attainment, culture, maturity with improvement methodologies such as Lean and Six Sigma and the number of operational 'flare ups' over time.

The deep dive revealed several key findings. The higher performing business units had several commonalities. First, both business units had Black

Attribute	Unit 1	Unit 2	Unit 3
Turnover	High	High	High
Significant Improvement Project Outcomes	Low	High*	High*
Black Belt Trained Leader	No	Yes	Yes
Goal Attainment (Service & Quality)	Low	High	High
Operational 'Flare Ups'	High	Low	Low
Culture (Pull vs Push)	Push	Pull	Pull
Lean Six Sigma Maturity	Low	High*	High*

Figure 7.6 Business unit showcase.

High = Above Average.

Low = Below Average.

* = Significant at 95% Confidence Level or Higher.

Belt trained leaders who amassed a respectable amount of significant improvement outcomes via projects using Lean and/or Six Sigma. They also matured with the methodologies over time. Their organizational cultures were geared more toward learning and proactive application of improvement skills versus waiting until the bonfire turns into a forest fire. The outcomes were significant at the 95% confidence level or higher.

As time progressed, these business units also improved quality and safety scores in light of market and industry challenges. These accomplishments are large in part due to the learning culture, proactive stance of the leaders and quest to achieve a culture of daily continuous improvement. Moreover, they experienced very few, if any, operational crises as compared to business unit 1. Simply put, units 2 and 3 were better run and experienced higher levels of process control. Thus, outcomes were elevated and sustained over time.

In contrast, business unit 1 did not have a Black Belt trained leader or a reasonable portfolio of improvement outcomes. The leadership cadre in this unit did have awareness of improvement methodologies such as Lean or Six Sigma, but never mastered the craft. This team was more reactive and waited for the fire to blaze instead of proactively addressing issues early on. This essentially mirrors a push culture where outside support was constantly being 'pushed' into the business unit to help solve crises instead of being 'pulled' in by the respective leaders proactively.

Thus, over 50% of the operational KPIs (key performance indicators) related to quality and safety were out of control consistently as evidenced by control charts and data trends. Also, this unit had experienced a several-year decline in quality and safety scores which worsened overtime. The chaos was displayed visually in both data and work areas. Overall, as outcomes declined operational 'flare ups' increased.

The pearl worth noting in Figure 7.6 relates to turnover. All three business units experienced above-average turnover for staff and leadership. Often, we hear leaders correlate (informally) turnover with declines in operational performance. Simply noted, often leaders espouse declines in goal attainment are attributed to higher levels of turnover. A simple correlation analysis was conducted which did not support this assertion. The correlation coefficient (r) was not even remotely significant when comparing turnover to quality scores as noted: Unit 1 ($r = .11$); Unit 2 ($r = -.38$); Unit 3 ($r = -.11$). In short, all three hospitals experienced high leader and staff turnover, but units 2 and 3 improved their quality and safety outcomes irrespectively.

When summarizing the findings, the change agent and team realized the operational 'flare ups' were chronic, increasing over time in scope and frequency and were not directly related to attributes such as re-sourcing or turnover. The most glaring root causes were leadership styles and a disconnect between process change and culture. The changes or 'fixes' for each 'flare up' did not stick because they were not aligned with the business unit's culture. Think of it as putting a band-aid on a ruptured artery. The band-aid may work for a very short time, but the bleeding will continue and worsen with time unless the wound is stitched properly.

The Response

The team crafted a road map that consisted of two channels. The first channel focused on any immediate issues that were a threat to life, safety or health. Once root causes were identified, teams of experts in various arenas were assembled and deployed to correct these issues. These teams spent most of their time at the Gemba (where the work was being done) in the unit listening, observing, rounding, connecting with staff, partnering for solutions, implementing best practices used by the other successful business units and auditing to ensure the solutions were effective. This channel was most definitely people and process focused. The corrections took several weeks, but produced noticeable and measurable outcomes that impacted thousands of customers favorably.

The second channel focused more on long-term solutions. The initial focus was to realign the business unit's culture with expected outcomes. To accomplish this, the team revisited the vision, mission and values to ensure leaders were aware of and modeling these fundamental attributes. The mission simply answers why we are here. The vision notes where we need to go. The values dictate what behavior is acceptable and expected by all staff and leaders in the organization. Values such as integrity and ownership were the focus in this turnaround.

In short, the team realigned the values to operations. Moreover, guardrails were added such as coaching, rounding and audits in partnership with the top leaders to ensure the changes 'stuck' long term. The goal was to reorient and recalibrate the top leader's behaviors and culture. Positive change must always start at the top.

Post change, the top leaders began to conduct regular rounds to connect with front-line staff, increase visibility, listen to their perspectives and use the feedback to course correct as needed. Also, outside experts from the other successful business units informally acted as onsite coaches to the business unit's top leaders to ensure the progress did not snapback once attention on the unit was diverted to other initiatives. Finally, regular audits were permanently conducted via mixed teams of the business unit's top leaders and outside experts to provide
an objective view point of progress or regression. The results were surprising, but favorable overall. The business unit turned the operational corner and began the recovery journey in spite of continued funding and turnover opportunities.

Lessons Learned

Looking back, the team gleaned several pearls from the case study and subsequent course corrections. First, perception is not always reality. As in this case, the struggling business unit's leaders perceived funding and high turnover to be the culprits of poor quality. In reality, this was not the case. Units 2 and 3 still performed at very high levels even though they experienced the same issues.

Second, culture is the real determinant of operational success or failure. As was learned in this situation, all leadership is not the same. For this cohort of business units, those top leaders who learned methodology and applied it regularly outperformed their underperforming counterpart significantly. The takeaway is that a proactive culture that improves daily is much better, effective and safer than one that waits until the fire overtakes the forest before responding.

Finally, leaders must close the loop and follow up regularly to ensure change 'sticks' long-term. Unit 1 had recurring snapbacks of operational failure when no one was looking. The team learned sustained long-term success was achievable with regular interdisciplinary rounding, direct communication up and down the organizational chart at the Gemba and audits to ensure the new reality became the true perception of top leaders. It can't be overstated: never take your finger off the operational pulse. Leaders simply don't know what they don't know. The best recipe to avoid a snapback is to assess, measure, round (at the Gemba), course correct real-time as needed and audit to close the loop. Closing the loop is the key to long-term sustainability of any process change.

Summary

As previously stated, change is the new normal. The only constant moving forward is change. Leaders, regardless of industry, must embrace, champion and leverage change proactively. Otherwise, the market and competitors will dictate your future.

The takeaway from the case study is that culture matters. Leaders are the bearers of organizational culture. Not all leaders are equally equipped to implement change successfully. As was displayed in Figure 7.6, leaders don't know what they don't know.

Improvement methodology really works if learned, deployed and supported by organizational culture and its leaders. The key is, for leaders, to proactively seek out opportunities to improve and transform organizational culture to one of daily continuous improvements. Otherwise, the alternative is consistent, recurring and unforgiving disruption. Look ahead, lean forward and strive to outpace the competition with time-tested and battle-proven methodologies such as Lean and/or Six Sigma.

Reference

1. Merriam Webster, 2021. https://www.merriam-webster.com/dictionary/change

The Art of Integration: The Basics to Successfully Merge Teams, Cultures and Organizations

Integration Defined

Integration is the 'incorporation as equals into society or an organization of individuals of different groups.'[1] In layman's terms, it's the art of pulling various stakeholders together to achieve a better end as a whole. There is an art and science to integrating different groups of people as they have various cultures, value systems, organizational structures and ways of doing business. Often, this concept is easier said than done and can produce unfavorable outcomes if not handled correctly.

Is the probability of success high or low with integrations? Is process more important than people when merging organizations? Can the small things prevent mergers from working? Are organization, communication and consistency keys to successful integrations? We will answer these and more in the following discussion.

I was introduced to this concept years ago as a young leader. Our organization of the time had a growth strategy in the pre-hospital emergency setting. In short, our leaders began growing a hospital-based ambulance service. The end goal was to create a large regional service that would provide high performing efficient emergency services to many hundreds of thousands of customers in a large geographic region. Moreover, the intended end was to improve, standardize and elevate services for the respective stakeholder populations by creating one service delivery model. Thus, eliminating variation and waste.

For a season, the team was charged with incorporating other competing ambulance services into our portfolio at a near-record pace. Former competitors became part of a larger team quickly. The leadership team created a simple template for these mergers. In short, the team focused on three basic fundamentals: people, structure and operations in this order. The key to note is that people always came first. As is often said, culture is the linchpin of strategy. If culture is not aligned properly, it will completely disrupt strategic plans.

Next, the team focused on structure. Essentially, leaders would determine the ideal organizational chart for the combined services and communicate this to stakeholders in the first phase of integration. The organizational chart was a

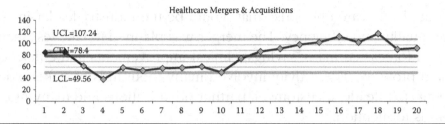

Healthcare Mergers & Acquisitions

Figure 7.7 Healthcare mergers & acquisitions control chart (Data Source: Reference 2).

clean and simple way of displaying where resources would be located, who reported to whom and who was in charge of what. This may seem to be inconsequential, but it's a very important tool for encouraging people to accept, understand and support change. It also helps to avoid chaos and confusion operationally speaking.

Looking back, these experiences went well overall. The key was simplicity and not over complicating the process. But, as with any change there were areas of improvement and growing pains. Were these experiences perfect? Absolutely not. Little did we know at the time, but these integration experiences were just the forerunner of many integrations the healthcare industry is experiencing today.

One of the most significant trends in healthcare currently is mergers and acquisitions. See Figure 7.7 for details.

In the last two decades, there has been a 57% increase in healthcare mergers and acquisitions.[2] These increases are significant at the 95% confidence level. Figure 7.7 shows a signal over the last nine years that this activity has increased due to an upward shift. Moreover, these mergers and acquisitions are technically out of control. The takeaway is that this activity has increased, the trend is likely to continue and more disruption is on the way.

So, why is this important to leaders? The majority of mergers and acquisitions eventually fail.[3] 'According to collated research and a recent Harvard Business Review report, the failure rate for mergers and acquisitions (M&A) sits between 70% and 90%.'[3] Regardless of industry, integrations of any form must be well planned, justified and executed flawlessly. Otherwise, the road ahead may not be the desired end.

Recently, a thought leader colleague shared an experience where an organization merged with a larger enterprise. The goal was to create a large multi-state healthcare enterprise that would be the industry leader in cost, service, quality and efficiency. The merger was planned to take less than two years and forecasted many savings, clinical improvements and efficiencies if executed properly. The activity involved many thousands of stakeholders including staff, leaders, customers, partner organizations and many more too numerous to mention.

Initially, the merger was structured well and execution was well thought out and planned. Think of the Kentucky derby. Dozens of world-class race-horses are lined up at the starting line held back by an individual gate in the stall. As soon as the gun is fired, the gates are opened and the race begins. The end game is the strongest horse wins.

Well, this merger was very similar. Many teams started the integration process and out of the gate it was an all-out sprint. A lot of progress was made initially, but challenges soon arose. As time progressed, some teams were front runners while others lagged behind. Shortly, the lagging teams began to experience confusion, communication conflicts and lack of di-rection. Instead of all the horses running to the finish line, some horses left the track for the stable and the integration process stalled. The end result was that several operational areas, morale declined, forward pro-gress came to a screeching halt and stakeholders simply didn't know what was the correct next step. Thus, the whole integration process was jeopardized.

In retrospect, the million-dollar question is, why? The thought leader espoused that the misfire with the lagging teams related to vision, roles and responsibilities, reporting structure and future road map ahead. In short, the integration process put the cart before the horse. These attributes were not an initial priority. The goal of the enterprise leaders was a soft-handed approach to integrate processes and technology first. Then, address structure and roles down the road at an undisclosed time. This misstep led to chaos, confusion, duplication of roles and many stakeholders backing out of the process.

The Blueprint

Successful integrations should focus on four basics to start: vision, form, function and efficiency. See Figure 7.8 for details. The first step in merging teams, cultures and organizations is to create the vision. A vision is, 'the ability to imagine how a country, society, industry, etc. could develop in the future

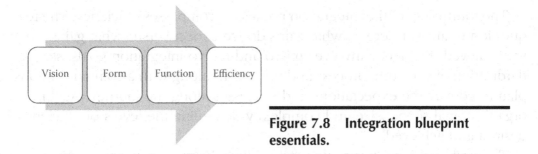

Figure 7.8   Integration blueprint essentials.

and to plan for this.'[4] In layman's terms, a vision is creating a visual display of where we are going together. Moreover, it outlines what success will look like and the desired end for merging the organizations.

Step two is to address form. Form essentially relates to roles, responsibilities and reporting structures. Establishing roles and responsibilities is greatly significant. This step tells stakeholders where they fit in the puzzle. Think of Maslow's hierarchy of needs. If people are fearful that they may not have a role or their basic ability to provide food, clothing or shelter will be impeded by the integration, they are more likely to resist the change. The goal is to get this elephant out of the room as soon as possible.

Form also encompasses reporting structures in the new organization. Common stakeholder considerations are as follows: Who will I report to? Do they have the experience, insight and political capital to help with my business unit? Will we be able to get along with the new leader as reporting structures change? Will the new leader support our goals, needs and current culture? These and many other thoughts need to be addressed by integration leaders so stakeholders have peace about where to find help when needed.

The third step in the integration process relates to function. Function in layman's terms relates to the integration road map. Integration leaders must layout a well thought out and crafted integration journey. This plan will include large and small tollgates with associated dates for each along the path.

Common tollgate examples include, but are not limited to, creating the vision, socializing the integration plan with stakeholders, designing the new organizational chart, merging technologies, measuring financial wins and the like. It's not uncommon to have hundreds and even thousands of tollgates along the journey. The key here is to celebrate success along the way and not overlook the small accomplishments. The end goal is to create a journey map to achieve measurable progress and outcomes that are significant.

The fourth step of the integration process encompasses efficiency. The real question to answer here is, what gains do we expect versus what gains have we achieved? Efficiency involves micro and macro integration goals, standardization of structure, process and operations along with a communications plan to convey the expectations and successes along the journey. Again, organizational scope, size and complexity determine the levels of efficiency desired and achieved.

The end goal is to ensure the end justifies the means. If an organization aims to save hard dollars, improve clinical services and create innovative access channels to thousands of customers, specific goals for each should be established and measured frequently. The true test of integration is if the enterprise's vision becomes a reality and the predetermined goals are achieved. Otherwise, it's simply changing for the sake of changing instead of a value add experience.

Pitfalls to Avoid

As noted in the previous example, there are several pitfalls to avoid during the integration process:

- **Lack of Vision**-As is written in Proverbs 29:18 (KJV), 'Where there is no vision, the people perish.' Step one for integration leaders is to create and socialize the organization's combined vision. Common considerations to include are what the combined structure looks like, whom the organization will serve, its operational footprint, where we are going together, the desired end and what success will look like at the end of journey. The biggest misstep for leaders is to start an integration journey without answering the basics first. Crafting a visual display of the journey that is simple, informative and measurable will help in this process.
- **Forgetting the Human Side**-All change requires human support, buy in and championship to be successful long-term. As noted in the previous thought leader example, integration leaders put the cart before the horse. They focused on technology and process before addressing the human side of change such as roles, responsibilities and reporting structures. Not answering 'where do I fit' is a major pitfall integration leaders must avoid early on. It's imperative that integration leaders

realize, plan for and mitigate unfavorable impacts on humanity. People are simply that: people. We all have personal obligations and life challenges. We work to positively impact humanity, help our organizations succeed and ensure we can provide basic life essentials to those closest to us. Integration leaders must put people first in the process or risk failure.

■ ***Disorder***-The third pitfall during the integration process leaders must avoid is disorder. In absence of order, there will be chaos, confusion and disorder. The quickest way to ensure integration failure is not having a well thought out plan, road map and tollgates to ensure forward progress. These plans don't have to be complicated or over analyzed. A visual display of the journey and desired targets along the way with dates will ensure disorder does not become the norm. Another crucial factor is communication.

Integration communications should be simple, clear, regular and hit the desired target audience. When people don't have answers, they simply create their own perceptions of what is or appears to be and this may lead to fear or false impressions. This pitfall can easily be avoided with a simple visual plan coupled with consistent and regular communications.

Summary

In today's world, change is the new norm and only constant. Thus, leaders must master the art of change management. Unfortunately, time has proven that most integrations will not be successful long-term.[3] Thus, leaders must strive and position themselves to be in the top 20%–30% of those that are successful. The only way to be successful in mergers and acquisitions is to put and keep people first.

As Peter Drucker has annotated, 'culture eats strategy for breakfast' or lunch. Without the support of people and aligning change with the organization's culture, strategy is only a concept without backing. Thus, the likelihood of integration success is low at best.

The takeaway is that change can be difficult and highly disruptive if not managed properly. The small things can prevent integrations from working on a grand scale. Organization, communication, consistency and leadership are imperative to ensure change works and stands the test of time.

In summary, leaders must master the basics to be successful on the big stage. The key to success is simply answering: Where we are going together, where does each stakeholder fit, where do I get help and what is success. Leaders who can master these basics, remain organized and communicate well, will position themselves and their organizations for integration success.

References

1. Merriam-Webster, 2021. https://www.merriam-webster.com/dictionary/integration
2. Kauffman Hall, 2020. https://www.kaufmanhall.com/ideas-resources/research-report/2020-mergers-acquisitions-review-covid-19-catalyst-transformation
3. https://businesschief.eu/corporate-finance/why-do-90-mergers-and-acquisitions-fail
4. Cambridge Dictionary, 2021. https://dictionary.cambridge.org/us/dictionary/english/vision

Chapter 8

Perspective: The Cardinal Sin of Failing to Look Back When Planning for the Future

Is All Disruption Bad? Case Study Approach to Determine Friend or Foe in Times of Change

The Value of Disruption

Is all disruption bad? Can a disruptor evolve into a friend or is it always a foe? Is it healthy for organizations to be disrupted frequently in order to see what's working versus what can be improved? Should organizations conduct after-action reviews for disruptors? Is the rear-view mirror helpful in determining the value of disruptors on business models? Is it possible to risk assess disruptors to determine the appropriate organizational response? These and other considerations will be answered in the following.

Disruption can be defined as, 'a break or interruption in the normal course or continuation of some activity, process, etc.'[1] In layman's terms, a disruptor is something or someone that changes the status quo. It is important for organizational leaders to consider several aspects of disruption. One, there are a couple of types of disruption. These include internal and external. Does the disruption affect internal operations, external operations or both? More discussion on this topic will follow.

Another lens of disruption relates to its impact on the business. The impact spectrum can range from departmental impact to the industry as a whole. Obviously, the greater the impact, the greater the organizational response.

DOI: 10.4324/9781003267966-8

However, it's important to note that even a disruptor that impacts a department or division of the business can have detrimental effects on life, safety, health and organizational mission.

Finally, leaders must consider the geographic reach of the disruption. The reach will determine the organization's response and availability of resources to help mitigate risks and return to a new state of normal post incident. Disruption geographical reach can span from local to international depending upon the issue.

Let's take a closer look at a case study where a large service organization assessed (in retrospect) the impacts of an international disruptor. The lens, viewpoints and impacts were surprising.

The Case Study

A large service industry conducted an after-action review of the impact of COVID 19 on its talent. There were two areas of focus: meetings and remote work. For the meeting's focus, the team selected a large meeting area that represented approximately 50% of the organization's meeting spaces annually. This pilot site was selected as a marker of significance. Did the pandemic significantly impact organizational meetings, interactions and produce both positive and negative outcomes?

Meetings View

A summary of the meetings study is summarized in Figure 8.1. The deep dive focused on meeting frequency, meeting duration, number of attendees and associated costs of meetings. Over the years, leaders have often said, 'This is an expensive meeting.' This analysis definitely provided context to this perception.

Pre COVID 19, the pilot site had 10,000 meetings per year in this location. It averaged over 800 meetings per month and 38 per day. The average meeting duration was 45 minutes with a group average of three people. Those in attendance were typically leaders of some sort.

The average meeting cost per hour was $675 and exceeded $5 million dollars annually. This pilot site accounted for over $400,000 of meeting expenses per month and nearly $20,000 per day. The study also revealed that this site's meetings averaged over 7,000 hours per year and 29 hours per day.

Meeting Attributes	Pre COVID 19	Post COVID 19 (1 Year Mark)	Difference	% Change
Number of Meetings Per Year	10,000	2,000	-8,000	-80%
Number of Meetings Per Month	833	167	-667	-80%
Number of Meetings Per Week	192	38	-154	-80%
Number of Meetings Per Day	38	8	-31	-80%
Average Meeting Duration (Hours)	0.75	0.5	0	-33%
Average Attendees Per Meeting	3	3	0	0%
Average Attendee (Leader) Hourly Salary	$225.00	$225.00	$0	0%
Average Meeting Salary Cost ($) Per Hour	$675.00	$675.00	$0	0%
Average Meeting Hours Per Year	7,500	1,500	-6,000	-80%
Average Meeting Hours Per Month	625	125	-500	-80%
Average Meeting Hours Per Week	144	29	-115	-80%
Average Meeting Hours Per Day	29	6	-23	-80%
Average Organizational Spend on Meetings Per Year	$5,062,500.00	$1,012,500.00	-$4,050,000	-80%
Average Organizational Spend on Meetings Per Month	$421,875.00	$84,375.00	-$337,500	-80%
Average Organizational Spend on Meetings Per Week	$97,355.77	$19,471.15	-$77,885	-80%
Average Organizational Spend on Meetings Per Day	$19,471.15	$3,894.23	-$15,577	-80%

Figure 8.1   Organizational meeting schedule assessment.

Post COVID 19 at the one-year mark, the team realized huge reductions in the number of meetings and in person meetings. As the pandemic disrupted every way of life, many staff and leaders were sent home for the year to work remotely. Moreover, a lot of the interaction, meetings and scheduled activity was cancelled due to other priorities. The outcomes were stunning.

Post pandemic, the meeting site realized an 80% reduction in meetings per year, per month and per day for example. The average meeting time decreased by 33%, but meeting attendance per group remained the same. The site also realized an 80% reduction in time spent per year, per month, etc., in meetings. The financial impact was over $4 million in labor saved for not attending meetings. Was this a value add? Short answer, most definitely.

The takeaway is that the disruptor (i.e., COVID 19) eliminated a lot of wasteful time and money spent on organizational meetings. The adage 'meeting for the sake of meeting' definitely applies here. The reality was that in the absence of in person meetings and significant expenditures the business kept running. Moreover, services (overall) were not stopped despite the new operating environment. In summary, the organization could and did do a lot more with a lot less.

Programmatic View

The team also 'plucked out' one of the organization's programs and studied driving time. See Figure 8.2 for details. The team comprises all onsite workers. When the pandemic arrived, the entire team was sent home to work remotely for an unspecified period of time. A few months turned into a year quickly.

Pre-pandemic, the team represented 1,300 work days per year which equates to 25 work days per week. This is calculated by measuring each team member individually. The average drive time per team member was one hour. For the team as a whole, the average drive time per day was five hours. Average team driving time per year totaled 6,500 hours and 125 hours per week.

At the one-year mark of the pandemic, the study revealed that the number of work days and work hours for the team was unchanged. Over the course of the year, the team drove 6,500 hours less because of remote working. This equates to over 500 hours per month and 125 hours per week. In retrospect, the team was more productive working remotely and the

	Pre-COVID 19	Post-COVID 19 (1 Year Mark)	Difference
Number of Work Days Per Year	260	260	0
Number of Work Days Per Month	22	22	0
Number of Work Days Per Week	5	5	0
Number of Work Days for the Team Per Year	1,300	1,300	0
Number of Work Days for the Team Per Month	108	108	0
Number of Work Days for the Team Per Week	25	25	0
Average Daily Driving Time Per Team Member (Hours)	1	0	-1
Average Daily Driving Time for the Team (Hours)	5	0	-5
Average Driving Time Per Year for the Team (Hours)	6,500	0	-6,500
Average Driving Time Per Month for the Team (Hours)	542	0	-542
Average Driving Time Per Week for the Team (Hours)	125	0	-125

Figure 8.2 Program assessment.

business continued to thrive in the new operating model. Simply put, the team spent more time on value add activity such as working instead of driving to and from the work site.

The organization learned that the pandemic was the ultimate disruptor. But, disruption is not always bad. Remote work provided the team with more autonomy, safety and time to work. It also saved tremendous amounts of money in travel expenses for the team.

The team saved over 150,000 miles in travel to and from work. This saved almost 8,000 gallons of fuel and over $23,000 in personal fuel costs. Moreover, the disruption of the norm saved over $15,000 for team in vehicle maintenance and repairs. The takeaway is that the disruptor added value to the team and organization in many ways.

The Risk Assessment

Once the team realized significant benefits from the disruption. They developed a risk assessment tool for this disruptor. It's imperative for organizations to under the impact of disruption on people, finances, operations and risk. See Figure 8.3 for details.

The disruptor risk assessment tool is a quick and easy guide for organizational leaders. The end goal is to determine the overall risk to the organization and its stakeholders so prevention and mitigation efforts are successful. Step one is to list the disruptors.

For step two, leaders assess each identified disruptor by the affects it will have on the organization and beyond. Will the disruption impact internal operations, external operations or both? Three, leaders score each disruptor based on the scope of business impact.

During this phase, it's important to consider if the disruptor will impact just a department, a division, the enterprise as a whole or the industry. It's important for enterprise leaders to also consider the geographic reach of each disruptor. Will the change of course be local, regional, national or international? The lens here depends on the disruptor. But the foci should be on how the organization at hand will be impacted as some organizations are regional or beyond in scope of services.

Fourth, leaders must consider the impact potential on people, finances and other attributes. Obviously, people come first. But, other considerations are warranted that may affect the organization's mission and long-term viability. The key is a broad lens to paint the best disruption picture.

Disruptor	Disruptor Affects 1. Both Internal Operations + External Operations 2. Internal Operations Only 3. External Operations Only	Scope of Impact on Business 1. Industry 2. Enterprise Wide 3. Divisional 4. Department	Geographic Reach 1. International 2. National 3. Regional 4. Local	Impact Potential 1. Impact People + Finances 2. Impact People 3. Other	Risk Score (Sum of Columns 2-5) *Lower Score = Higher Importance
COVID 19 (Talent Management Focus)	1	1	3	1	6
Local Water Main Break	1	3	4	1	9
IT Ransomware Attack	2	2	3	1	6

Figure 8.3 Disruptor risk assessment tool.

Finally, the tool scores the risk to the organization as noted in the figure. The lower the risk score in the model indicates a greater organizational response is required.

Let's take a closer look at a practical example. In Figure 8.3, the COVID 19 pandemic was the first disruptor listed. It scored high on its impact on both internal and external operations. It also impacted the entire industry and had an international impact. The pandemic impacted both people and finances of the organization. Thus, a high-risk score was assigned.

Let's compare this to another example in the figure. A local water main break had significant effects on the business, but was limited to a division of the organization. Its geographic reach was local, but its impact potential was focused on people and finances. Think of it as a local hospital where the water main breaks. Thus, the surgery center is temporarily closed for the day. The impacts will be on both people and revenue streams. However, the organization can quickly pivot as the water main will be fixed within 24 hours. Thus, the risk is less than the pandemic.

The key is for leaders is to thoroughly assess, analyze and score risks to the organization and its stakeholders. Disruption is not always bad, but it can be deadly to the business model if not acted upon correctly.

Summary

As noted, change is the new norm and only constant. Thus, risk will grow with time. The million-dollar question is how will enterprise leaders identify, assess, score and mitigate their risks. Visionary leaders will succeed in handling risks. While their counterparts will become victims of the subsequent disruptions.

We learned in the case studies that not all disruption is bad. As with risk, disruption has both an upside and downside. The upside is associated with some level of benefit. In contrast, the downside is synonymous with cost or negative impact.

Disruption can be an operational friend in some instances. However, leaders will have to ensure these realized benefits are magnified with proper analysis and visual display. Otherwise, the negative aspects will take precedent and create the perception that disruption is on a foe. Thus, the diamond in the rough will never be discovered.

Finally, the key to change is being prepared to manage its affects. Change management is by far often overlooked and underappreciated until the next crisis appears. Change agents should always value the rear-view mirror perspective. Often, it's hard to appreciate every aspect of change when the organization is driving 100 mph. But, the after-action review is a great tool to capture the positive in often very negative circumstances.

The key takeaway for leaders is to view disruptors from various lens and focal points. The key to success is knowing when to respond to and when to magnify disruption. In short, always magnify the good, minimize the bad and learn from each change.

Reference

1. Merriam-Webster, 2021. https://www.merriam-webster.com/dictionary/disruption

Chapter 9

Exclusivity: The Cardinal Sin of Being So Inclusive that It Becomes Exclusive

Case Study: Is It Possible for Inclusion Programs to Become Exclusive? When Diversification Effects Become Siloed & Ineffective

One of the hottest topics in industry today is diversity and inclusion. What does this really mean? Will creating diverse teams always ensure success, synergy or improved outcomes? What does a diverse team really look like? Is there a magic ratio of diversity that ensures success? Will all efforts of diversifying the organization, leadership cadres or teams last long term? Are there critical factors that determine how successful diverse teams and leaders will be? We will answer these and other questions in the following dialogue.

The purpose of this case study is to summarize the efforts of several organizations to diversify their organizations, leadership teams or programs. Moreover, the end goal is to identify themes that resulted in both successes and failures on the diversity journey. The desired outcome for each organization was to improve something. It's important to note that each organization is a service provider of some sort serving many tens of thousands of customers in diverse and significant geographic service areas. Thus, critical leadership and programmatic decisions essentially affect life, health and safety of great pools of humanity.

DOI: 10.4324/9781003267966-9

Diversity can be defined as, 'the condition of having or being composed of differing elements.'[1] Another view of diversity is, 'the inclusion of people of different races, cultures, etc. in a group or organization.'[1] This concept is synonymous with the term variety. But, is only focusing on race or culture a short-cited view? The short answer is most definitely in some cases.

When considering organizations, leadership teams and programs, diversity can be applied to race or culture. However, the concept also is much broader. It includes diversity in world view, experience, business experiences, skill sets, education, training and gifting just to name a few. The takeaway is that the outward appearance of a person is not what makes the person. One's world view is compounded from years of life experiences both on and off the job. This view of how the world works varies geographically, by age bracket and in some instances based on financial background.

Experience is another diversity factor. In healthcare, for example, a diverse skill set comprises operational experience, clinical experience and performance improvement experience with significant outcomes is greatly prized and the new leadership paradigm. The key here is experience tied to significant outcomes that impacted humanity in great ways. These experiences also help create cultural competencies and individual world view.

Finally, diversity in education, training and gifting cannot be overlooked. The adage 'one trick pony' applies here. In today's world, change is the only constant and new normal. Environments plagued with constant and disruptive changes eventually produce high levels of risk. Thus, organizations and their leaders must invest, prize and reward talent for knowing more not less. The key is that the more leaders and their teams know, the better suited they will be to handle change and successfully mitigate risk. One trick ponies will simply not stand the test of time in today's disruptive leadership and organizational environments.

A compliment to diversity is inclusion. This concept can be defined as, 'the act or practice of including and accommodating people who have historically been excluded.'[2] Again, the first knee-jerk reaction is to focus on race or some other like demographic. But again, what about including other attributes such as training, skills, experience dealing with difficult changes and the like. Focusing on demographics is a very short cited approach that will prevent organizations and their leaders from reaching their full potential.

To further assess this topic, let's take a closer look at four case studies in the service industry.

Case Studies

Organization A

A few decades ago, a group of local public servants in the fire and law enforcement professions realized certain demographics were not proportionately represented in their departments as a whole or in the leadership ranks. Thus, the response was to form a union. Then, seek legal counsel and file a discrimination lawsuit.

The claim was that both departments lacked minority representation that mirrored the communities served. At the time, the communities were represented by approximately 40% minorities. This trend held for several decades. In comparison, the command staff for one of the service agencies had 0% minority representation. The end goal of the lawsuit was to force the local government to increase leadership diversity and include more minorities at all levels.

The result of the action was historic. A federal judge ruled that the service agency had to hire and promote essentially quotas of minorities in various classes until the department and leadership makeup represented that of the community. Shortly after, the department leaders began the diversity journey. They began hiring and promoting a disproportionate amount of minority public servants to meet the quotas.

With time, the majority group felt they had been unfairly treated and passed over for long-awaited vertical opportunities. The response was the creation of a union. The union's creation resulted in a waterfall of complaints and formal grievances which stalled the federal judge's order. For years, the two sides battled it out with grievances and lawsuits over hiring and promotion practices.

The battle came to a head with a reverse discrimination lawsuit filed by the majority party. This group won the lawsuit and received back pay, wages, promotions and the like. The government was forced to hire outside consultants to complete promotion assessments and eventually create a new promotion system based on qualifications instead of demographics. The process took years and eventually cost the local government and its tax payers millions of dollars to resolve.

The end game was that a tidal wave of promotions and power shifts went in the favor of the majority party at the end of the battle. This trend persisted for years and still is the norm. Simply put, they were more skilled and

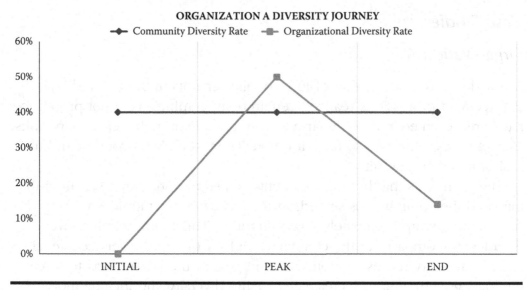

ORGANIZATION A DIVERSITY JOURNEY

Figure 9.1   **Organization A diversity journey.**

performed better on competitive promotion tests than their minority counterparts in many instances. Thus, the local government depended on an
independent promotion system to determine its leaders to avoid subjectivity.
The government reverted back to the basics of hiring and promoting based
on qualifications instead of other demographic factors.

It's interesting to note a couple of trends. See Figure 9.1 for details. During
this several decade period, the community diversity rate was approximately
40% minority and maintained at this level. In contrast, the public service
department's diversity varied.

Initially, the department's command staff (i.e., top leadership team) had
0% diversity. After years along the diversity journey with initial lawsuits,
grievances, unions and the like, the departments command staff was 50%
diverse. This was higher than the community rate. At the end of the journey,
the command staff diversity rate was 14%. This was mainly due to attrition and
retirements in which the majority party increased its representation through
the qualifications based promotion system.

The takeaway is that the organization and its stakeholders perceived a
problem existed. Two, various parties acted to address the perceived problem. Three, the actions had long-lasting consequences for all stakeholders.
Four, the diversity gains were not sustained long-term. However, the agencies
were more diverse in the end than in the beginning.

Organization B

Organization B began a diversity journey aimed at a group of top organizational leaders. The goal was to diversify its top leadership group responsible for services provided to many tens of thousands of customers annually. These leaders represented operations, support services and essentially every aspect of running a large corporation. With each decision point, great pools of humanity would be impacted in even greater ways. So, those trusted to lead the organization were crucial to life, health and safety of many.

When the journey began, the national average diversity rate for this leadership group and industry was 14%. This rate maintained as the standard throughout the journey. The national average was the benchmark used by the enterprise to determine success or opportunity to be addressed. In contrast, the organization's diversity rate for top leaders was initially 0%.

After several years of diversity planning and execution of those plans, the diversity rate hit an all-time high of 30%. This level of diversity lasted a few years with slow, but noticeable declines. See Figure 9.2 for details. Most of the gains in diversity were attributed to top leadership direct appointments which conflicted with the traditional promotion process for the organization.

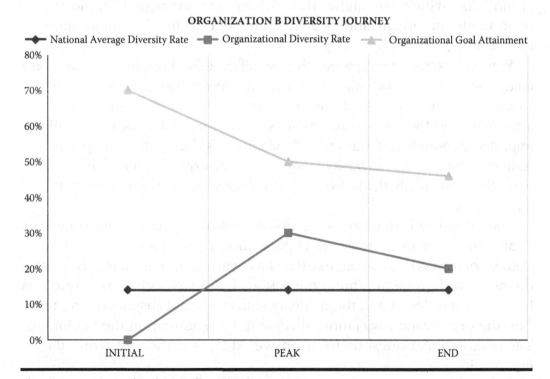

Figure 9.2 Organization B diversity journey.

Historically, vacant leadership positions would be posted publicly for a period of time. All qualified applicants would then receive an interview to vie for the role. The interviews typically were panel interviews consisting of various leaders and interested parties based on the open role. Then, the most qualified applicants would be chosen.

During this time frame, direct appointments became the norm and created organizational challenges. Not all staff and leaders supported or respected the new process for a variety of reasons. One, the new process conflicted with the organization's hiring and promotion policy. The norm quickly became 'do as I say, not as I do' which did not resonate with thousands of staff and leaders. Moreover, many of the leadership appointments clashed culturally with organization values. Thus, the organization's culture, particularly around high-quality services, quickly washed away. The result was detrimental operational decline.

In Figure 9.2, when the diversity journey began the organization's top leadership cadre was 0% diverse and operational goal attainment tied to service, cost and quality was approximately 70%. As time passed, diversity increased to 30%. But, the operational goal attainment declined to 50%. At the end of the journey, diversity rates for top leaders settled around 20% which was higher than the national average. But, more importantly the organization's goal attainment declined to an all-time low of 46%.

You may be wondering why this is significant. In short, the organization's culture was washed with all the leadership appointments. Thus, operational successes of the past eroded quickly. These declines in operational goal attainment cost the enterprise hundreds of millions of dollars and negatively impacted hundreds of thousands of stakeholders during the time period. Although the intent to diversity leadership in this organization was noble, execution was highly disruptive and in the long run was very costly in many ways.

The takeaway is that both Organizations A and B had a similar genesis related to the diversity journey. Organization B and some of its stakeholders perceived a problem existed. Two, various parties acted to address the perceived problem. Three, the actions had long-lasting consequences for all stakeholders. Four, the diversity gains were not sustained long-term. But, the organization was more diverse in the end than in the beginning. The million-dollar question to be answered is, 'was the cost worth the end result?'

Organization C

Organization C began a diversity journey by creating a new highly prized program in the service industry. This organization was a large service provider and impacted many hundreds of thousands of customers annually. The intent was to create an incubator of sorts. This operational incubator was designed to house diversified cutting-edge talent, create new ways of doing business, redefine how this particular service industry would operate in the future and simply rewrite the industry's book of knowledge.

The goal was to create a historically new prototype for diversity, staffing management and innovative outcomes. In terms of diversity, leaders used several KPIs (key performance indicators): national average diversity rate for the industry, community diversity rate and organizational diversity rate for the program. Each KPI was measured initially when the program was started. Then, at increments represented in Figure 9.3 by the program's peak and end measurement. The intent was to use this as a template to increase diversity rates throughout the enterprise. The desired end was for the organization to mirror the community diversity rate and later national trends.

At the program's start, the diversity was 0% as this program was the first of its kind in the organization's history. The team building efforts quickly assembled a team representing various segments of the world and was 78% diverse at its peak. With time, the program experienced challenges and

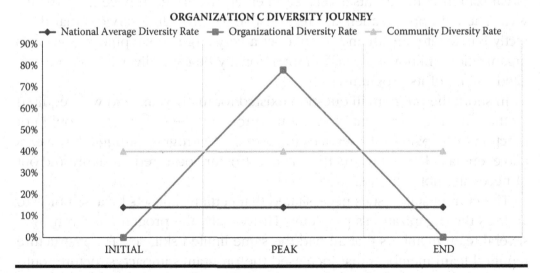

Figure 9.3   Organization C diversity journey.

eventually did not survive. Thus, the team was dispersed, the gains in diversity were lost and the diversity rate returned to 0% for the program.

There were several reasons the program failed. One, the team assembled was extremely different from the organizational norm in terms of skill sets, philosophy, world view and culture. The organization as a whole struggled to connect its purpose and mission to the program's work. Two, the change that emerged from the program's structure was immediately radically different and disruptive. There essentially was no 'honey moon period' between the program and organizational leaders. Thus, leaders and stakeholders were thrust into a scenario of 'shock and awe' instead of being acclimated slowly to the new operating environment. The key is that the intent was good, but execution was not aligned properly with people, culture and outcomes. Thus, it was short lived.

The takeaway is that Organization C had a similar genesis to Organizations A and B related to the diversity journey. Organization C and some of its stakeholders perceived a problem existed. Two, various parties acted to address the perceived problem. Three, the actions had long-lasting consequences for all stakeholders. Four, the diversity gains were not sustained long-term. Was the risk worth the investment long term? In short, arguably not.

Organization D

Organization D represents a very large enterprise in the service industry as well. The enterprise leaders are responsible for providing services that directly impact life, health and safety over a very large geographic region. This organization unknowingly and unintentionally began a diversity journey related to one of its programs.

In short, the program in question existed for many years and was required by the federal government. Without the program, the organization could not function or be paid for its services rendered. The program struggled for years and eventually led to a restructure. The restructure occurred suddenly and out of necessity, not a choice.

The current state issues necessitated that certain skill sets be assembled to address the organization's problems. Historically, the program was run by several team members that all had the same limited skill set. The restructure required team members that increased the program's impact, structure, outcomes and capabilities by 75%. Simply put, the new program structure was

75% more complex than its original structure and rewrote the industry book for best practices.

Post restructure, the program quickly became a star (operationally speaking). The team produced historical outcomes that directly impacted the safety and effectiveness of hundreds of thousands of customers annually. Soon after, the program became a national best practice site and began to impact the industry's body of knowledge. Success quickly evolved from a pipe dream to a daily reality.

When the team was restructured, it was 75% diverse meaning 75% minority. This far exceeded the community diversity rate of 40% and the national diversity rate of 14%. See Figure 9.4 for details. At the program's peak, the team diversity rate fell to 60%. At the end measurement, the team was 50% diverse and maintained this level for many years. This was the new normal and operational 'sweet spot.'

In retrospect, Organization D was similar to the other organizations in some ways. But, very different in others. Similarly, Organization D perceived there was an issue that need to be addressed. Then, crafted an action plan that was executed quickly which had large scale long-lasting effects.

The plan not only ensured diversity of people, but more importantly and primarily focused on diversity of knowledge, skill sets, experience and outcomes. The team was able to achieve the synergistic effect of doing more with less by leveraging team strengths found in diversity. Simply put, the diversity

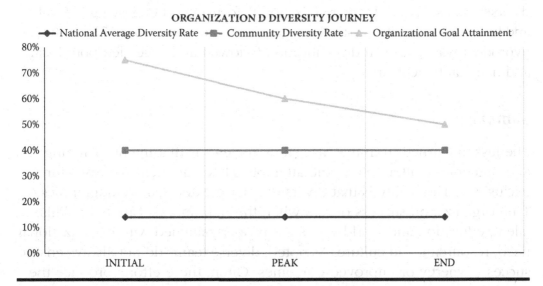

Figure 9.4   Organization D diversity journey.

in capabilities increased by 75% post restructure. Thus, the organization's success sky rocketed as well.

The byproduct of the diversity journey was a diverse team in terms of demographics. In contrast to the other organizations, Organization D's primary focus was on the big picture. This global focus was laser focused on ensuring all customers received high-quality low-cost services when and where needed versus socially engineering based on demographics. The end most definitely justified the means and was worth the investment in multiple ways.

Common Themes

The common themes from the case studies are as follows. One, all organizations perceived a problem existed. Two, the leaders invested time, money and other resources in action planning to address the perceived problems. Three, all organizations implemented plans that had long-lasting effects on great pools of humanity. Four, each plan produced consequences whether desired or not.

Moreover, 75% of the organizations did not reach or sustain their diversity goals long term. In contrast, Organization D did achieve and exceed its diversity goals. The glaring difference was that three of the four organizations were focused solely on primarily diversifying people pools to reach certain quotas or diversity benchmarks. The key takeaway was that the greatest diversity gains emerged by Organization D focusing on improving life, safety and health of humanity versus demographics of team members. The fortunate byproduct was that team diversification followed and exceeded both local and national benchmarks.

Summary

The lesson learned from the case study reviews is that intent, planning and outcomes matter. Often, the attempt to become inclusive results in exclusivity. The reality is that diversity is far greater than demographics. True organization success occurs when the right mix or variety of skills, talent, education and world views are properly aligned with organizational need, resourcing and culture. As noted, diverse teams do not always ensure success, synergy or improved outcomes. Often, these efforts produce the exact opposite.

Finally, there is no magic ratio of diversity that ensures success. Unfortunately, as noted, not every effort to diversify organizations, leadership cadres or teams will last long term. The critical factor to success is implementing the journey for the right reasons. The ultimate end goal should be to improve the life, health and safety of humanity versus solely focusing on other demographic attributes.

References

1. Merriam-Webster, 2021. https://www.merriam-webster.com/dictionary/diversity
2. Merriam-Webster, 2021. https://www.merriam-webster.com/dictionary/inclusion

Chapter 10

Waste: The Cardinal Sin of Not Recognizing the Elephant in the Room

Is Organizational Waste a Risky Proposition?

The Value of Eliminating Waste

Waste is, 'an unnecessary or wrong use of money, substances, time, energy, abilities, etc.'[1] The term is synonymous with value add or subsequently non-value add. In layman's terms, value is anything a customer is willing to pay for.[2] In contrast, any activity that produces waste or erodes value to the customer is a non-value add.[2]

Historically, thought leaders have focused mainly on the financial impacts of waste for example. One of the most common questions leaders have posed to change agents is: 'Is the presence of waste in operations a negative force on the organization's bottom line?' The key here is bottom line which connotes the organization's finances. For years, this has been the driving force of waste elimination efforts.

This impact traditionally mainly focused on hard dollar or soft savings. Hard dollar savings are those that result in a tangible dollar savings from reducing waste. In contrast, soft savings are those that provide an improvement. However, do not have a direct tangible dollar savings tied to them.

In today's world, change is the new normal and only constant. As change increases, so does its associated risks. Per Merriam Webster, risk is the 'possibility of loss or injury.' In reality, the goal is to minimize or marginalize risk at every turn. Thus, leaders should move beyond the traditional view of waste's impact and try a new lens.

The most common view of waste refers to the eight wastes taught in traditional Lean or Six Sigma programs.[2] The eight wastes consist of several attributes such as defects or errors, producing more than the customer's needs, waiting (i.e., delays), non-utilized talent, wasted motion, excessive inventory, transportation and extra-processing.[2] The key here is that waste is bad and must be eliminated. The whole premise is that organizations and their people spend time doing things that ultimately do not add value to the customer.

Years ago, a large health system began a journey to high performance. The enterprise had a large regional footprint and provided services to hundreds of thousands of customers annually. One aspect of the journey was to train several cohorts of top leaders in Lean Six Sigma. The initial intent was to transform these leaders into master change agents. With the newly acquired process improvement skills, the organization's focus was on identifying waste and addressing it quickly. The initial focal point was hard dollar savings.

With time, the organization evolved into a master training site. Thus, many dozen top leaders successfully completed Lean and/or Six Sigma courses. Then, they were turned loose on the organization to solve the 'world's problems,' so to speak. The train and deploy model was used here. Unfortunately, the organization as a whole did not adopt the methodology and engrain the skill sets into organizational norms. The training for most simply became another plaque on the wall and another credential for the resume.

At one point, a top-performing change agent conducted an independent study of the organization. This change agent had many significant successes with the methodology and knew it would work anywhere. In a first pass, the change agent began looking horizontally and vertically for the eight wastes. In a short time, the top performer fund over $40 million in process-related waste. Shortly after, the list of waste grew to over $100 million.

The adage 'measure twice and cut once' applies here. These findings were presented to hundreds of top organizational leaders in a public venue. The responses were all over the spectrum. For moments, one could have heard a pin drop. The responses were synonymous with the phrase 'jaw dropping.'

The lesson learned is leaders don't know what they don't know. Also, they don't know what they don't measure. The organization's elephant in the room was over $100 million in process-related waste. The problem was that ignorance seemed bliss. The leaders only focused on the dollar potential of waste.

What about the other risks? The waste also directly impacted service, quality of services, safety and effectiveness just to name a few. The organization was experiencing significant challenges with customer satisfaction rates over time for example and struggled to answer why. The answer was simple. It was the waste that was plaguing the organization at every turn.

The key here is that waste is multidimensional. Yes, waste has financial implications. However, other risks must be considered to paint the full picture. There are several questions thought leaders and their organizations must consider:

- Does waste matter?
- Is organizational waste impactful on the organization and its stakeholders?
- How much waste exists in the organization?
- Can waste be risk assessed?
- Does all waste pose the same risk level to organizations?
- Is the risk of organizational waste only impactful to the organization or can it spill over into other geographic arenas?
- What is the risk potential to the organization due to the presence of waste?
- What high-risk wastes are the biggest risk to the organization?

These are just a few starter considerations. But, the key is that waste and risks are bad. Thus, leaders and their organizations must assess the level of waste, risks and their impacts on the enterprise and its stakeholders. Otherwise, ignorance is bliss and disruption is just around the corner.

Let's take a closer look at a few practical examples of waste and how organization's risk scored their waste. Was the waste a campfire or forest fire waiting to explode? Let's see.

Risk Assessing Waste

The following are a few real examples in the healthcare industry. It's important to note that these concepts will apply to any industry. The focal point is the tool, process and outcomes. Not necessarily the content or specific examples.

The first step is for leaders and change agents to identify organizational waste. Then, score each waste issue based on several attributes. The first two indicators of risk noted relate to scope and reach. For organizational scope, it's important to consider whether the waste impact is enterprise wide, divisional or department specific.

Geographic reach is similar. The question here relates to if the waste's reach is national, regional (to the organization) or local. The response here will depend upon the organization's scope and size. The key is the greater the waste's reach and scope, the greater the risk for the enterprise and its stakeholders.

Next, leaders must consider the impact of waste and its disruption potential. For impact, it's important to consider if the identified organizational waste directly or indirectly impacts the customer. Also, is the waste highly disruptive to operations, the organization as a whole and the service delivery capabilities to customers? The greater the impact and disruption potential equates to higher risk levels to the enterprise.

Finally, the tool assesses waste based on benefit potential and risk level overall. There are several questions to consider as it relates to benefits of addressing the waste. Does elimination or mitigation of the waste immediately benefit life, safety and health? Do these responses immediately benefit the organization's mission? Are successful risk mitigation efforts important, but have no direct impact on life, safety, health or mission? The key here is that the greater the benefit of waste elimination, the higher the risk score.

In comparison, the risk level score is predicated on a similar scale as noted in Figure 10.1. The key here is that the higher the risk to life, safety, health and mission, the greater the risk. This high-risk waste deserves and necessitates top organizational priority. Thus, leaders must know their risks imposed by organizational waste and mitigate them appropriately.

Let's take a practical look at Figure 10.1 and the noted examples. Figure 10.1 lists several examples of organizational waste. A brief summary of each follows:

- ◾ *Lab Testing Delays*-A large healthcare organization had its own internal core lab. The lab was a very high-volume operation and processed hundreds of thousands of tests annually. At one point, the lab experienced significant delays in processing critical tests. This was a direct risk to thousands of customers. A team was formed and successfully

Waste Issue	Type of Waste	Organization Scope 1-Enterprise Wide 2-Divisional/Entity 3-Departmental	Geographic Reach 1-National 2-Regional 3-Local	Impact 1-Directly Impacts Customer 2-Indirectly Impacts Customer 3-No Impact	Disruption Potential 1-High 2-Medium 3-Low	Benefit Potential 1-Immediate Benefit to Life, Safety, Health 2-Immediate Benefit to Mission 3-Important, but not an immediate Benefit to 1 or 2	Risk Level 1-Risk to Life, Safety, Health 2-Risk to Mission 3-Important, but not a risk to 1 or 2	Risk Score *Sum Columns 3-8 Lower Score = Higher Risk	Risk Level
Lab Testing Delays	Delay	1	2	1	1	1	1	7	High Risk
Emergency Response Times	Delay	2	2	1	1	1	1	8	High Risk
Program Staff Utilization	Non Utilized Talent	1	2	2	2	2	2	11	High Risk
Team Member Utilization	Non Utilized Talent	1	3	2	3	2	2	13	Low
Document Work Flow Delays	Delay	1	2	2	1	2	2	10	High Risk
Manual Document Management System Process Delays	Delay	1	2	2	1	2	2	10	High Risk
Emergency Treatment Delays	Delay	2	3	1	1	1	1	9	High Risk
Change Agent Utilization	Non Utilized Talent	1	2	2	2	2	2	11	High Risk
Avg Score Risk Level		1.3 High Risk	2.3 Low Risk	1.6 High Risk	1.5 High Risk	1.6 High Risk	1.6 High Risk		

Max Risk 6
Lowest Risk 18
Avg Risk 12

Figure 10.1 Outlines a waste risk assessment tool.

mitigated these risks. Thousands of delays were eliminated and found to be statistically significant.

- **Emergency Response Times**-A large regional ambulance service experienced delays responding to emergency calls. Think of strokes, heart attacks, car wrecks and the like. This service responded to tens of thousands of emergency calls annually. Thus, many lives were affected by this waste. A team of change agents were deployed for resolution which resulted in the saving of tens of thousands of emergency response times annually and significant cost savings. As a result, many lives were saved and the impact on humanity was immeasurable.

- **Program Staff Utilization**-A significant program tied to safety and effectiveness of services was underutilizing talent. The team was overwhelmed and focused thousands of hours annually on activities that did not provide value to customers. A team was deployed for an assessment and solution. The findings were significant. The team was spending 70% of its time on non-value add which cost the organization hundreds of thousands of dollars annually in non-utilized talent. A course correction ensued and the team quickly became a national best practice site, accomplished more with synergistic foci and significantly improved safety and effectiveness of services for hundreds of thousands of customers.

- **Individual Team Member Utilization**-A significant program tied to provision of services was asked to do more with less. In essence, find ways to better utilize each team member. Without this program, the organization could not function. A change agent was deployed for a time study and found a diamond in the rough. One role was not utilizing its talent 80% of the time. This cost the organization tens of thousands of dollars annually in waste. A course correction was made and productivity levels were elevated to the industry standard.

- **Document Work Flow Delays**-A service organization relied on documents such as policies to create standard work for many thousands of workers. These documents ensured work was done correctly each and every time. Thus, eliminating errors, reworks, delays in service and the like. At one point, a team realized there were tens of thousands of work flow delays as documents were being processed for revisions and approvals. The team implemented several automated solutions such as reports, automated e-mails to stakeholders and the like. In short order, the delays were quickly eliminated, significant and resulted in improvements in service and quality of services.

- *__Manual Document Management System Delays & Non-Utilized Talent__*-A large service organization used outdated technology to manage its policies, procedures and the like. This system was a quasi knowledge management system that ensure a standardized approach to doing work for thousands of workers. It also was a well of knowledge for all stakeholders to locate the organization's interworkings and knowledge as to how work is done in every area of operation. This was key to continuity of services. It was discovered that the system, its manual processes and those that used the system were wasting significant time during transactions. A team was deployed and saved thousands of hours annually by eliminating the manual processes and subsequent delays. The financial savings addressing these issues was in the hundreds of thousands of dollars annually.
- *__Emergency Treatment Delays__*-A hospital realized hundreds of customers annually were experiencing delays in care. In the emergency world, every minute counts. Thus, a team was assembled to find a solution. The team course corrected quickly and reduced hundreds of emergency care delays in the first year alone. The subsequent impacts spilled over into an enhanced revenue stream and improved community relations. The impacts on quality, service and financials were significant.
- *__Change Agent Utilization__*-A large service organization invested in Lean Six Sigma training for hundreds of leaders and staff. The initial focus was on cost savings. Later the foci evolved to improving quality, services, value and the like. Post training, enterprise leaders realized over 90% of those trained never utilized the credential. Moreover, the return on the investment in hard dollar savings was only 10% of the projected return. The investment overall was a non-value add and non-utilized talent was ramped. A course correction ensued, but the organization only improved the return ratio to 30%. Thus, millions of dollars were left unaccounted for and waste remained a constant threat to the organization.

Synopsis

So, what's the moral of the story? Each example previously noted identified some form of waste and implemented a solution. Some of the solutions were effective, statistically significant and stood the test of time. All issues, in one way or the other, affected the customer. But, there is still remove for improvement.

There is something missing from the analysis. Not one of the organizations assessed its risk as it relates to waste. The main focus of all initiatives was financial improvements primarily and others were nice to have. Let's look closer at Figure 10.1.

If leaders risk assess each waste, over 60% of the issues were related to delays of some sort. The remaining waste was primarily tied to non-utilized talent of some form. Of the waste listed, 88% is high risk as noted in Figure 10.1. The only low-risk waste is the individual team member as it relates to better using time. Is waste a risky proposition? Simply put, yes.

On further inflection, leaders should also assess risk for the assessment attributes in Figure 10.1. Out of six attributes, only one was low risk. This relates to geographic reach. Each waste imposed regional or local implications only. Thus, the low-risk score was indicated.

In terms of organizational scope, 75% of the waste impacted divisions of each organization or the enterprise as a whole. Needless to say, waste had a significant impact on the organizations and its customers. For customer impact, the waste in all categories impacted the customer in some way. Thirty-eight percent of the waste examples directly impacted the customer. Thus, a direct and expedited organizational response is warranted for these high risks.

In terms of risks and benefits of addressing the waste, 100% of the wastes impacted life, safety, health and the organization's mission. Each one of the waste examples had some effect on the organization's future direction. Thus, this is more evidence that waste is risky and must be addressed accordingly.

Summary

The moral of the study is that waste does matter and is very risky. Organizational waste impacts people, organizations, stakeholders and is most definitely the elephant in the room much of the time. The only question is how many leaders can see the elephant, weigh it and understand its risks?

The adage 'we don't know what we don't measure' is definitely relevant. Leaders must understand the concept of waste. Moreover, change agents are critical to ensure organizations identify, measure, analyze and address waste-related risks. Ignorance is never bliss. What organizations and their leaders don't know will eventually harm them and their customers in one way or the other.

The traditional model of viewing waste from a cost savings perspective only is short cited, not practical and very dangerous. The reality is that change is the new norm and no signals have emerged to show the trend is slowing anytime soon. As change increases, so will its associated risks. Thus, leaders must use simple risk assessment tools to understand their organization's risk as it relates to waste.

In summary, waste can also be compared to a poisonous snake. A common phrase many use all the time is, 'if it was a snake, it would have bit you.' This connotation relates to something being close to someone, but they fail to see it for one reason or the other. The key takeaways are as follows. Waste is important, impactful and bad. One derivative of waste-filled environments is risk. Risks are significant, dangerous to the operation and need immediate attention. Leaders must gain a new perspective of risk and its impacts. Otherwise, the new phrase will be, 'it was a snake and it bit you.'

References

1. Cambridge Dictionary, 2021. https://dictionary.cambridge.org/us/dictionary/english/waste
2. IISE, Lean Green Belt. 2016.

Conclusion

The takeaway is that risk is everywhere. It can be very dangerous to organizations or a motivator if leveraged properly. We learned that ignorance is never bliss. Change is the new norm. As change evolves and grows, so do associated risks.

For leaders to succeed in high-risk environments, they must be able to identify disruptors early. Where risk is prevalent and a threat to the organization, prevention, mitigation and marginalization of risk affects is a good starting point. The key is for leaders to be proactive instead of waiting for risk to knock on the organization's front door.

The takeaway is risk is a reality not just a mirage. Risk applies to all industries and businesses. Not everything is high risk. Some organizational attributes are lower risk. Thus, leaders must plan and respond according to the risk level.

Moreover, it is possible to predict the future (to some degree) by risk assessing the current environment. The adage 'past behavior is a good predictor of future behavior' is relevant here. Risk is an equal opportunity offender. It affects organizations, leaders and customers all the same.

The key is for leaders to be knowledgeable. The reality is that leadership perception is not always reality. If knowledge is lacking, leadership ignorance eventually will cause organizational disruptions and even failure if not corrected sooner than later. As we learned, risk is applicable to planning, time, value, knowledge, vision, conflict, perspective, inclusion efforts and waste.

The ultimate cardinal sin of leadership can be summed up simply: Leaders don't know what they don't know, leaders don't know what they don't measure.

If organizations and their leadership cadres can measure, analyze, plan, look forward, see the diamonds in the rough, magnify their strengths to minimize weakness and view risk through multiple lenses, they will succeed in high-risk environments. If not, the journey ahead will be one filled with constant disruptors, potholes and undesirable organizational outcomes.

Index

Note: Page numbers followed by "f" indicate figure.

Printed in the United States
by Baker & Taylor Publisher Services